T0268109

Alpine Elixirs

*Whether milk, Most or merlot...
here's to my favorite drinking buddies,
Sam and Stella*

Bergli is being supported by the Swiss Federal Office
of Culture with a structural grant for the years 2021–2025.

Alpine Elixirs
The Swiss Art of Quirky Cocktails, Cozy Coffees,
Mouthwatering Milkshakes and More

Text and photography: © Andie Pilot, all rights reserved.
Additional photos pp. 6 (top), 14, 28, 50, 56, 60, 63, 92, 114, 150 © Samuel Bucheli;
p. 78 (top) © Daniel Ammann; and p. 91 © Distillery Studer, photos by: (middle right)
Gian Marco Castelberg; (top right, middle left, bottom row) Sebastian Magnani
Illustrations, layout, and typesetting: Elżbieta Kownacka
Editor: Angela Wade
Proofreader: Karin Waldhauser

ISBN: 978-3-03869-159-4
First edition: May 2024
Printed in the Czech Republic

© 2024 Bergli Books
An imprint of
HELVETIQ SA
Mittlere Strasse 4
4056 Basel
Switzerland

bergli.ch

FSC
www.fsc.org

MIX
Paper from
responsible sources
FSC® C014138

Alpine Elixirs

The Swiss Art of
Quirky Cocktails, Cozy Coffees,
Mouthwatering Milkshakes and More

by Andie Pilot

A Schümli Pflümli

Table of Contents

Introduction

My name is Andie Pilot and I like to drink.

Luckily, I live in the right country for that.

In Switzerland you can drink water straight from a mountain spring, wine from some of the world's most beautiful vineyards, beer on top of a mountain, *Schnaps* made from everything from hay to pine boughs to edelweiss, and milk almost directly from a cow's udder.

My journey to make this book has taken many years and many tipples.

I grew up in Canada but visited my Swiss family every summer before moving here in 2010. As a child on holiday, many of our daily activities revolved around going somewhere and then having a drink. We hiked up a mountain then downed a Rivella (the national soda), or swam in a lake then fueled up on ice tea. At breakfast and dinner we drank cold milk and chocolate powder, shaken together in plastic cups with screw-top lids designed just for this purpose. Meanwhile, my mother and aunt drank *Milchkaffee* (coffee with warm milk). They had coffee after lunch, too, with a spot of cream—my cousins and I clambering for the lid of the little plastic pot (more on those collectible lids on page 41). Even after we returned to Canada, my mother made us warm Ovomaltine (Ovaltine) on dark winter evenings, which we drank before bed.

When I moved to Switzerland as an adult, I tasted the other side of Swiss drinks—gaining a great appreciation for Swiss wine and enjoying the best craft beers from outstanding Swiss producers like BFM. Out on the slopes I had my first *Schümli Pflümli*, a warm, boozy coffee, topped with mountains of cream that made me feel like I could keep skiing forever. My sister-in-law, who works at a distillery, gave me a wonderful introduction to Swiss spirits; and not just kirsch, but a whole array of fruit brandies. From there my love only grew.

I wrote my first Swiss drinks book, *Drink Like the Swiss*, in 2018. This new version expands on my previous work with photos and more recipes. In the past three years, I also had the great pleasure of meeting numerous Swiss producers, many of whom are featured throughout this book.

Whether hard or soft, creamy or tart, sparkling or still, I hope this book inspires you to try some new Swiss drinks or gives you a better understanding of your old favorites.

So, let's raise our glasses! *Proscht! Santé! Viva! Salute! Zum Wohl!*

Cheers!
Andie
Trubschachen, Switzerland, 2024

But wait... *do* the Swiss drink?

The famous French Renaissance philosopher Michel de Montaigne wrote in his essay "On Experience" (*De l'expérience*) published in 1580:

> "You make a German ill if you force him to lie on a mattress, as you do an Italian on a feather bed, or a Frenchman without bed curtains or a fire. A Spaniard's stomach cannot tolerate the way we eat, nor ours the way the Swiss drink."

> (*Vous faites malade un Aleman de le coucher sur un matelas, comme un Italien sur la plume, et un François sans rideau et sans feu. L'estomac d'un Espagnol ne dure pas à nostre forme de manger, ny le nostre à boire à la Souysse.*)

The Swiss were notorious heavy drinkers during Montaigne's time and although this reputation has faded, a rich drinking tradition continues throughout the country. Those who think of the Swiss as mild mannered and temperate have never been to *Fasnacht* in Basel, a *Fête de Vendanges*, or a meeting of pretty much any Swiss student fraternity or football club.

But it's not just about booze. The Swiss are not only brewers, vintners, and distillers, they are also coffee dealers, dairy farmers, and ice-tea fanatics. Whether it's syrup made from elderflower blossoms, caramel *Schnaps* as a reward for the back-breaking labor of making linen by hand, a sweet-cherry love potion made by farmers' daughters and served to bachelors on New Year's Eve, or heavily spiced wine pouring out of a fountain to ring in the New Year, the Swiss tie drinks and drinking to all aspects of daily life and celebration.

You, too, can drink like the Swiss!
The intention of this book is to provide an overview of Swiss drinks and drinking habits. There are traditional recipes from grandmothers and farmers, classic cocktails with a Swiss twist, and new drinks using the best ingredients that Switzerland has to offer.

Each of the drink recipes in the book serves one, unless otherwise noted. The recipes were developed using the metric system and the imperial measurements vary slightly.

Rules for Raising Glasses

I was threatened with seven years' bad sex the first time I drank before I "cheers-ed" at a Swiss party. In Canada it's no sin to drink before a toast, but in Switzerland there are a few rules that define the ritual of raising a glass.

1. Once you receive your drink you must not take a single sip until the toast is over and everyone has clinked glasses.
2. Make eye contact while you clink.
3. Say the person's name as you clink.

It may seem overly formal, but this acknowledgement of your fellow drinkers is a way to show respect to the host and other guests. Whether you say *Proscht*, *Zum Wohl*, *Santé*, *Salute*, or *Viva*, Swiss drinks are definitely worth the ritual.

Boozy Terminology

There can be some confusion as to what constitutes *Schnaps* and brandy, especially when comparing European varieties to varieties sold in the English-speaking realm.

The cherry "brandy" and peach "schnapps," from my misfortunate early days of drinking in Canada, are actually liqueurs, heavily sweetened and flavored, with a lower percentage of alcohol (around 15-30%).

The word *Schnaps* in German refers to any strong, distilled spirit. Similarly, the word brandy really means a spirit distilled from wine (though there are fruit varieties, which are labeled as such). Although *Schnaps* and brandy can be flavored, they typically have a higher alcohol content (around 40%).

Any mention in this book of *Schnaps* or brandy refers to the higher proof, European variety. The higher sugar varieties are referred to as liqueurs.

In French, *eau-de-vie* refers to any strong spirit, while in Italian it's *distillato* or *acquavite* and in German *Branntwein*.

Drinking Vessels

To drink well, you need the proper vessel. In Switzerland, a land of practicality and order, there are numerous cups, glasses, mugs, and tankards that correspond to most liquids.

Mostbecher

Apple cider, known in German-speaking Switzerland as *Most*, tastes best when it's poured into salt-glazed ceramic jugs and mugs. This beautiful grey pottery with sweeping blue designs is perfect for keeping your cider impossibly cold and protected from the light (which can dull its flavor).

Zinnkannen/Pichets d'étain

You'll find these pewter jugs and matching cups in secondhand shops, the display cases of municipal buildings and *Gasthofs* (country inns), and the vitrines of elderly relatives and neighbors. They are often engraved to commemorate special events such as sporting victories or long service to a company or organization. *Zinnkannen/pichets d'étain* would traditionally have been for serving wine, but today they are mostly decorative, and different regions have different shapes and styles.

SIGG bottles

Ferdinand Sigg, son of a foundry man, founded an aluminum manufacturing company in 1908 in Biel, eventually producing everything from bicycle license plates to egg slicers to toy cash registers. However, his most famous design was a simple, lightweight aluminum water bottle, which became the iconic "face" of the company. It was even included in the collection of the Museum of Modern Art in New York. Sigg died in 1930 and the company was taken over in 1936 and again in 2016, but the bottles still bear his name and mark his legacy.

Boccalini

A hundred years ago, mammas and nonnas in the Italian-speaking Swiss canton of Ticino didn't keep their meat and wine in a fridge, but in a grotto (cave). Cool and constant, the grottos' temperature made them perfect storage facilities. With a stone table at the entrance, they also became the perfect meeting place to set the world to rights over a glass (or two) of wine. These grottos eventually evolved into restaurants, where the wine was served in small ceramic mugs called *boccalino* (plural *boccalini*). If you were traveling in Ticino and wandered into a grotto, you could have your wine plain or with a splash of Gazosa (see page 19). When you were finished, you could buy the little *boccalino* as a souvenir of your trip.

Glass from the forest

Today, if you are looking for decorative glassware in Switzerland, your best bet is Glasi Hergiswil. They make bowls, platters, glasses, and ornaments directly connected to Switzerland's long tradition of glassmaking.

References to Swiss *Glashütten* (buildings where glass and glass products are made) date back as early as the 13th century, but the most notable glassmakers were a trio of brothers originally from the Black Forest. They were given permission by Lucerne's government in 1723 to manufacture in Flühli, a heavily forested settlement in the Entlebuch region in central Switzerland.

But why Flühli?

This idyllic little town was sparsely populated, and although it would eventually become a beloved tourist destination, it was hardly famous. It did have one thing going for it—wood. To make glass you need an extremely hot fire, which of course demands incredibly large amounts of wood as fuel. The dense forests around Flühli were perfect for this.

The brothers came from a long tradition of glassmakers and the kinds of glass that they made in Flühli—coloured glass, painted glass, intricate blown forms—were unique and sought-after. Their designs are still favored by today's collectors, who pay big money for the rare pieces.

Their business expanded rapidly as demand grew, but soon the effects were felt: the forests were thinned out, and the Entlebuchers feared the loss of their wood and the erosion of the exposed ground. The glassmakers needed to find a new place, which they did in Hergiswil, on the shores of Lake Lucerne, in 1815. Over the next 50 years they split the production with the Entlebuch, eventually moving to the new factory for good in 1869.

Today the glass products of Hergiswil are an important reminder of this long tradition in central Switzerland. For a great day out, you can visit the factory in canton Nidwalden, which features a museum, glass labyrinth, and the opportunity to blow your own glass ornaments.

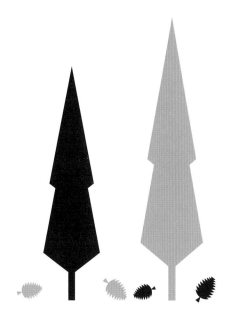

Canärli

At the end of a meal in Switzerland in the 1960s or 70s, you might have seen a little crystal duck on the table, called a *Canärli*, which is a play on the French word for duck (*canard*). Ladies would pour kirsch into its hollowed out back, dip a sugar cube into the alcohol, then let it slowly dissolve on their tongues. This was a digestif, or maybe a *Bettmümpfeli* (a little treat before bed).

Marketed to the fairer sex—"you can drink and remain a lady!"—it eventually fell out of favor. Today, you can still often find the colorful or clear glass ducks at Swiss secondhand shops or hear reports about traveling seniors' groups having a quick *Canärli* on their tour bus.

The rest of the group boarded the gondola and rode up to Männlichen. From Männlichen, they then hiked to Kleine Scheidegg after an obligatory *Canärli* refreshment stop.

fricktal24.ch

On Saturday morning, over 60 singers made their way to Niederurnen. Strengthened by a *Canärli* in the car and a coffee on site, we arrived at the rehearsal venue in good time for the sing-along.

Katholischer Kirchenmusik-Verband des Kantons Luzern

As soon as we set off, Katja and Martina served the popular *Canärli* (kirsch on sugar cubes), a tradition that no trip is complete without.

Aargauerzeitung

We enjoyed the ride through the Lower Engadine. Finally we had our first *Canärli*... Most of the brave ones grabbed one!

Trachtengruppe (folk group), Baar

For a few senior citizens, the time was just right to take a short afternoon nap. But their tired minds were soon awakened with a *Canärli*.

Seniorenreise (seniors' trip), Boningen

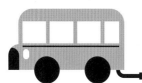

Dog grog

And which Swiss drinking vessel is the most famous of them all? Probably the little barrel hanging around the neck of a Saint Bernard.

Although the dogs likely never carried flasks around their necks, it became an essential part of their folklore. The dogs lived at the top of the Great St. Bernard Pass in a hospice first documented in the 11th century. It was run by monks and often used as a refuge for travelers. The St. Bernards, as they would eventually be called, lived there from the late 1600s on and were great rescue dogs, bounding proudly through the snow to find weary travelers and guide them to safety.

The persistent myth of the rum-filled flasks was likely started when Napoleon crossed the Great St. Bernard Pass with his troops in 1800. One of his soldiers wrote home to his mother about the helpful dogs which lived at the top of the mountain and provided weary travelers with "*eau-de-vie* that hangs from their collars." A few years later the French writer, Anne-François-Joachim Fréville, who had written a book about famous dogs, described it as a flask, filled with brandy, on a chain around the dogs' necks to revive snow-bound travelers. A famous painting also helped spread the idea of brandy-toting dogs. "Alpine Mastiffs Reanimating a Distressed Traveler," by Edwin Landseer (who was only 18 when he painted it), shows the hospice dogs—one with a barrel around its neck—coming to the aid of a man buried in the snow. This vision of the Alpine Mastiff, later known as the St. Bernard, has become synonymous with the breed and they continue to be portrayed as such today.

Although the dogs did carry provisions in sacks, the story of the brandy-filled receptacle around their necks was rejected by the monks; nevertheless, they did keep little barrels available for tourists who wanted a photo with a brandy-carrying St. Bernard.

BOTTOMS UP!

The most famous Swiss rescue dog is Barry. Born in 1800, this very good boy managed to save more than 40 people during his service at the hospice. You can learn more about his life (and see his taxidermied body!) at the Natural History Museum in Bern.

If live St. Bernards are more your thing, check out Barryland. This breeding center in Martigny, canton Valais, tells the history of the breed in Switzerland and shows its impact on the culture—plus there are plenty of puppies to pet!

Top left and bottom right, Scuol; top right, Funtana Carola, and bottom left, Büvetta Tarasp, all in canton Graubünden

Chapter 1:
From the Springs

Water is the basis for all drinks. The Swiss like to drink their water plain and still, which is more popular than sparkling. According to the Association of Swiss Mineral Springs and Soft Drink Producers, the Swiss consumed around 110 liters/29 gallons of mineral water per person in 2022.

Switzerland is awash with mineral-rich wells, sometimes springing from deep in the mountains. Initially it was doctors and apothecaries who used this kind of water therapeutically and, when not prescribing it plain, experimented by adding different curatives and flavorings, resulting in the creation of many soft drinks.

The temperance movement in the early 20th century helped promote the consumption of non-alcoholic beverages over liquor, and from the 1950s onwards, mineral water and soft drinks, as well as juice, were seen as healthy alternatives to alcoholic drinks.

Mineral Spas

In the 1800s, Switzerland was a hub for Europe's upper classes, who attended to their health at one of the 350 natural mineral spa resorts. Although people had been bathing in these healing waters for centuries, by the late 1800s these health retreats claimed to treat everything from anemia and anxiety to rheumatism and rashes.

And it wasn't just about bathing in the waters, though that was an important part of the treatment. Guests were also encouraged to drink many of the regional mineral waters to help cure their ailments. Different regions had different minerals in their water, like sulfur, iron, magnesium, and zinc, which were imbibed according to the maladies of the guests.

The spa tourism boom lasted up until the First World War. Although there are still plenty of popular spas to visit today, like Leukerbad and Bad Ragaz, many resorts that once counted as the most important in Europe, like Fideris in canton Graubünden, have disappeared.

BOTTOMS UP!

Spa towns like Scuol in Graubünden have different mineral springs boasting different mineral properties. Today, you can visit Scuol's mineral spa as well as go on a mineral water walk which allows you to taste the water from different springs—some of which come carbonated, directly out of the town's fountains.

Philippus Theophrastus Aureolus Bombast von Hohenheim
otherwise known as:

Paracelsus

Switzerland's most famous alchemist was born at the end of the 15th century in Egg, a small village near the abbey of Einsiedeln. He spent much of his life wandering through different communities, speaking to everyday people, railing against the medical establishment, and practicing as a doctor and alchemist. With so much wandering, it's almost unbelievable that in his 47 years he managed to write countless volumes on medicine, chemistry, the natural world, and even magic—in his time he was the second most prolific scholar after Martin Luther.

Paracelsus encouraged doctors to better observe their patients and was a proponent of an evidence-based approach to medicine. He was skeptical of bloodletting and denounced the practice of applying cow paddies to heal wounds in favor of keeping them clean.

It was also Paracelsus who created laudanum, brought chemistry into medicine, and gave us the words chemistry, gas, and alcohol—which he borrowed from Arabic. *Al* simply meant "the" and *kohl* was the powdered essence left over after sublimating stibnite, which had been used as a cosmetic for centuries, notably in dark eye makeup. The *kohl* was essentially the spirit of the substance, just like high-proof alcohol was the spirit of distilled wine.

As an alchemist, Paracelsus was also interested in *Aurum Potabile* (drinkable gold), thought to be the universal curative and possibly the elixir of life.

Guldenwasser

The *Little Bernese Cookbook* from 1749 has a recipe for *Guldenwasser*, a dilution (both in name and substance) of "gold in water," or as Paracelsus thought, a cure-all. According to the cookbook, a tablespoon of this spirit on an empty stomach would awaken the brain, cure vertigo, open the lungs, ease labor pains, and more.

I've updated the recipe here, taking out some impossible-to-find and possibly poisonous ingredients (I'm looking at you, creeping ivy), and can confirm that it does awaken the brain (and back of the throat).

GULDENWASSER

About 5 g/0.2 oz each of galangal, ginger, grains of paradise, lavender, long pepper (pippali), nutmeg, sage, and turmeric
5 juniper berries
5 cloves
3 bay leaves
2 cinnamon sticks

Place the aromatics in a 1 liter/33 fl oz bottle, cover with kirsch or another clear spirit, and leave in a warm place for at least two weeks. Strain into a bottle and add 4 tablespoons of sugar or sugar syrup. Shake well until all the sugar has dissolved.

Swiss Soft Drinks

Switzerland has its fair share of home-grown soft drinks. On average, the Swiss drank around 66 liters/17.5 gallons of soda per person in 2022, according to the Association of Swiss Mineral Springs and Soft Drink Producers. Here are some of the most famous.

Rivella
Of course, the national soda pop of Switzerland is made with milk.

First produced in 1952, Rivella is one of Switzerland's most iconic drinks. Its name is a mix of the Italian word *rivelazione* (revelation) and the Ticino town of Riva San Vitale. It's made from milk serum (also known as whey), herb and fruit tea extract, water, and sugar.

Whey is what makes the drink particularly Swiss. For centuries, dairy farmers enjoyed drinking this byproduct of cheese production, and later it was adopted as a health product by early Swiss nutritionists. In the 1800s, health tourists to Swiss sanatoriums took whey baths.

The whey that's used in today's Rivella is more processed than the unfiltered product of the past. However, much like another famous Swiss drink, Ovomaltine, its connection with overall health, outdoor life, and so-called nutritional benefits are still heavily promoted.

These days, if you are at a restaurant and you order Rivella, your server might ask you "red or blue?" Red is standard, while blue is the low-calorie option, and uses artificial sweeteners. Although the company has experimented with many flavors, including rhubarb, peach, lemon, mango, mint, pomegranate, and a green version with green-tea extract, as well as versions with or without carbonation, the standard red and blue have remained constant throughout the years.

In 2008 they launched Rivella Yellow, a drink with soy serum that they collected as a byproduct of tofu manufacturing. Accessible for vegans, it was also easily digestible for anyone with a milk intolerance. After underperforming on the market, it was discontinued in 2011.

Gazosa
These colorful, flavored sparkling waters from Ticino have been around since the end of the 19th century. Called "poor man's champagne," because the bottles made a similar pop when opened, Gazosa initially relied on natural fermentation to create its bubbles. Today the flavors—everything from indigo Alpine blueberry to bitter orange—are simply added to carbonated water.

Pepita

Switzerland's grapefruit soda has been around since 1949. The water used to make the drink comes from the springs at Eptingen, near Basel, one of the deepest mineral springs in the country. According to Eptingen themselves, they have the most minerals of the Swiss mineral waters, with an especially large amount of magnesium and calcium.

Vivi Kola

Launched in 1938, Switzerland's first cola had a map of Africa on the label, indicating the country of Cameroon, where the Kola nuts used to flavor the drink purportedly came from. Mixed with spring water from Eglisau in canton Zurich, the cola became popular first with the Swiss troops, who drank it as an alternative to beer, then with cycling fanatics after it sponsored the Tour de Suisse in 1949. Although the company shuttered its doors in 1986, it was revived in 2010 and continues to be produced today.

Elmer Citro

Elmer Citro is Switzerland's best known lemon-flavored pop. Its recipe has not changed since 1927, when production began at the Elm spring in canton Glarus. The water from Elm spring had been bottled and bathed in since the Middle Ages, and it remains the exclusive source of water for the Elmer Citro drink.

Schweppes

None of these drinks could have existed without the ingenuity of inventor Johann Jacob Schweppe, who used the research of Joseph Priestley to develop a practical process to add bubbles to drinks. His company Schweppes was founded in Geneva in 1783.

Ice tea

Check any Swiss *Badi* (local swimming pool), and you're bound to find ice tea bottles or tetra packs scattered next to nearly every towel.

Ice tea, and particularly the variety sold from the supermarket chain Migros, has been a cult Swiss product for over 30 years; yet, before the early 80s, ice tea wasn't available commercially. After tasting ice tea on a trip to the United States, Ruedi Bärlocher decided to brew a batch and test it with the Swiss populace. With partner Max Sprenger, their initial production of 2000 one-liter/34 fl oz tetra packs hit the shelves. The Swiss loved it.

Today, the Swiss remain the largest consumer of ice tea in Europe, guzzling around 30 liters/8 gallons per person per year (compared to the next highest, the Belgians, who consume only about 10 liters/2.6 gallons). Migros alone produces around 60 million liters/16 million gallons a year in a variety of flavors—from Alpine herbs to rhubarb—though the original version remains the favorite.

LE PAMPLEMOUSSE

50 ml/1.7 fl oz gin
30 ml/1 fl oz lemon juice
15 ml/0.5 fl oz elderflower syrup
Pepita (grapefruit soda)

Shake together the gin, lemon juice and elderflower syrup with ice. Strain into a glass. Top with Pepita.

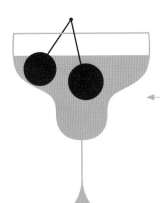

HEIDI

Like a Shirley Temple (she famously played Heidi, after all) but with a Swiss twist.

1 tbsp grenadine or raspberry syrup
Elmer Citro

Pour the syrup over ice in a glass. Top with Elmer Citro and stir. Garnish with a cherry. To make a Heidi's Grandfather, make a Heidi and spike with kirsch.

RIVELLUM

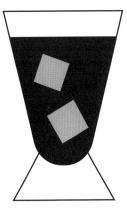

60 ml/2 fl oz rum
30 ml/1 fl oz lemon juice
120 ml/4 fl oz Rivella

Stir with ice, then pour into a glass.

BLUEBERRY FIZZ

50 ml/1.7 fl oz gin
30 ml/1 fl oz lime juice
1 egg white (optional)
Blueberry Gazosa

If you are using egg whites, shake the gin, lime juice and egg white in a cocktail shaker first without ice, then add the ice and shake again (this creates the best foam). Otherwise, just shake with ice. Strain into a glass and top with blueberry Gazosa.

Sirup

Go to any Swiss cafe with a small child and they will probably be offered a glass of *Sirup*—a concentrated sugar syrup topped with still or sparkling water. The flavors vary, but *Sirup* remains a firm favorite with children and adults alike.

You can buy the concentrated syrup in most places—from local farm stores to supermarkets—but it's also quite easy to make at home. The basic proportions are 1:1 sugar to liquid. The procedure simply involves heating the mixture until the sugar dissolves, then straining and bottling.

Here I have outlined a few varieties, but the flavor possibilities are endless (and you'll find Switzerland's favorite syrup, elderflower, on page 26). Small batches can be funneled into clean bottles and kept in the fridge for a couple of weeks. If you plan to keep it longer, or out of the fridge, you'll need to use sterilized bottles (either directly from the dishwasher or placed in boiling water for 10 minutes) and a bit of citric acid to help preserve it (about 30 g/1 oz per liter of liquid).

When the sugar dissolves in the water, the final quantity is about 75% of the original volume; for example, if you use 200 g/7 oz liquid and 200 g/7 oz sugar, that leaves you with around 300 g/10 oz syrup.

BOTTOMS UP!

Switzerland's most famous syrup producer is probably Distillery Morand in Martigny, canton Valais. The company has been producing syrups and spirits since 1889, and became especially known for their Williamine, an *eau-de-vie* made from the Williams pear.

You can buy their products throughout the country, and their range of syrups is really something to marvel: from violet to verbena, cassis to crème brûlée, mint to melon—they have flavors for every occasion. They even offer syrup made exclusively from Valais fruit.

Want to try for yourself? Visit their lovely shop in Martigny where they have an extensive syrup tasting bar.

FRUIT SYRUPS

You can make cooked or uncooked varieties.

Cooked: cook the fruit to extract the juice, strain well, then add an equal part sugar, heat until dissolved, then bottle.

Uncooked: puree the fruit, strain well, add an equal part sugar, heat until dissolved, then bottle.

Great fruits to use: cherries (recipe below), raspberries, plums, strawberries, apricots, quince, etc.

CHERRY SYRUP

400 g cherries
100 ml/½ cup water
Around 300 g/10 oz sugar

Add the cherries to a pot with the water (no need to pit).

Cook over medium heat for about five minutes, or until the cherries start to break down and you can squash them with a spoon.

Using a fine mesh sieve (and some cheesecloth if you have it), strain the cherry juice into a measuring cup. You should have around 300 ml/10 fl oz of juice.

Add an equal amount of sugar (if you indeed have 300 ml/10 fl oz, add 300 g/10 oz sugar), then heat the mixture. As soon as the sugar has dissolved, pour it into a clean bottle. This keeps in the fridge for about a week.

AROMATIC SYRUP

You can use all kinds of herbs and spices to make aromatic syrups. Dissolve sugar in an equal part water, add the aromatics and let cool. Strain and bottle.

Great aromatics to use: cinnamon (recipe below), rosemary, vanilla, and star anise.

CINNAMON SYRUP

250 ml/1 cup water
250 g/1 cup sugar
4 cinnamon sticks

In a pot over medium heat, cook the water and sugar until the sugar has dissolved. Take off the heat and add the cinnamon sticks. Cover and let cool. Strain into a clean bottle and keep in the fridge for a couple of weeks. Makes 375 ml/1½ cups.

ALPINE ICE TEA SYRUP

You can use this as a base for ice tea (just dilute with water to your desired sweetness), or use it in mixed drinks and punches in place of sugar syrup.

500 ml/2 cups water
Juice and peel of 2 lemons
   (remove the peel carefully,
   avoiding the bitter white pith)
4 Alpine herb tea bags
2 black tea bags
Sugar

Place the water, juice and peel in a pot and bring to the boil. Reduce heat and add all the tea bags. Simmer two minutes, then remove the black tea bags, then simmer an additional five minutes. Remove the remaining tea bags and lemon peel. Weigh the remaining liquid, then add an equal part sugar and simmer until it has dissolved completely. Strain into a bottle. Let cool then store in the fridge.

WINE SYRUP

If you have leftover wine, you can easily cook it into a wine syrup, which is lovely for cocktails, or adding sweetness to *Glühwein* (mulled wine). Simply heat equal parts wine and sugar over low heat (keep it low to preserve the flavor of the wine) until the sugar dissolves. Then strain and bottle.

Red, white or rosé work great. You'll want to use light wines like fruity Fendant or peppery Pinot— nothing heavy or aged in oak.

Elderflower Syrup

Elderflower syrup (*Holunderblütensirup/sirop de sureau*) is a particular favorite in Switzerland. It's added with abandon to desserts, sparkling water, wine, or cocktails like Hugo, for a light and floral taste of summer.

Tips for picking the blossoms

Elderflowers start to bloom in late May or early June, depending on the year and your region. There are plenty of elderflowers growing along the edges of forests and paths along rivers. You'll be able to see, and smell, when the blossoms have just opened and are ready to be picked.

Before you go foraging, make sure you have everything ready at home for syrup-making, as you want to process the flowers as soon as possible. It's best to pick on a warm, dry day, and the earlier in the day the better. Look for freshly opened buds and use scissors to cut off the bunches of blooms. Don't place them in plastic bags, as they will wilt, but rather in an open basket.

ELDERFLOWER SYRUP

About 10 stems of elderflower blossoms
1 kg/2.2 lb sugar
1 liter/4 cups water
1 lemon, sliced
30 g/1 oz citric acid (see below)

Gently shake any bugs off the elderflower stems.

In a large pot, cook the water and sugar until the sugar has dissolved. Remove from heat, add the lemon, citric acid and the elderflower (flower first, stems sticking up—the stems shouldn't touch the syrup as they are bitter, or you can also cut them off) and then cover with the lid of the pot.

Let sit for 24 hours.

Line a strainer with cheesecloth and set it over a large pot. Pour the syrup through, discarding the blooms and lemon. Bring the liquid to a simmer (it should reach 85°C/185°F) and then funnel into sterilized bottles. Keep the bottles in a cool, dark place. Once you open a bottle, it should be kept in the fridge. Makes about 750 ml/3 cups.

• Citric acid is available in big supermarkets and drugstores and it helps preserve the syrup, as well as adding a little extra tang. If you make a smaller batch and plan to use the syrup quickly (within a couple of weeks), citric acid is not necessary, though the bottle should be kept in the fridge.
• Sterilize your bottles by running them through the dishwasher, or placing them in boiling water for 10 minutes.

Chapter 2: From the Pastures

One enduring vision of Switzerland is the mountain meadow—wildflowers gently swaying in the wind or being slowly munched on by calm, curious cows.

Dairy farming makes up a fifth of Switzerland's agriculture, and the Swiss consume on average about 60 liters/16 gallons of milk per person per year, according to the *Schweizer Milchproduzenten SMP* (Swiss milk producers association).

The country has excellent infrastructure to bring the milk, their white gold, to the masses. There are pipelines transporting it directly from cows in Alpine pastures to processing plants below, and plenty of dairies in Switzerland have their own milk vending machine where you can get pasteurized or unpasteurized milk directly from the dairy, sometimes 24 hours a day. Milk is consumed domestically, as well as exported both in liquid and powder form.

Taking the cows up to the Alps in the summer and letting them graze on fresh Alpine meadows has a positive influence on the flavor of Swiss milk. But that's not the only reason the milk tastes so good.

Switzerland has some of the strictest animal welfare regulations in the world, and the farms are regularly inspected. On average, each farm has only around 23 cows, making it easier to take care of the animals and to spread them comfortably across the available land.

According to Identitas, Switzerland's animal registry, as of February 2024, the top names for cows were:

French:	German:	Italian:
1. Bella	1. Bella	1. Luna
2. Tulipe	2. Fiona	2. Stella
3. Etoile	3. Sina	3. Bella
4. Noisette	4. Bianca	4. Tina
5. Iris	5. Nora	5. Perla

Bovine Beauties

Switzerland's favorite animal is the cow. Whether it's the bashful Brown Swiss from the eastern side of the Brünig-Napf-Reuss line*, or the mottled Simmental found to the west, there's a soft spot in every Swiss heart for these lovely, long-lashed ladies.

The average Swiss cow lives on a small farm, spends her days munching grass in the pastures and mooing at passersby. Each day she eats about 100 kg/220 lb of meadow grasses, 2 kg/4.4 lb of feed, 200 g/7 oz salt, and drinks 50 liters/13 gallons of water. From that, she produces about 20–25 liters/5–6.5 gallons of milk.

And when she has calves of her own, according to my veterinarian father-in-law, Robi, she will be rewarded with one of the Swiss farmer's treasured drinks: *Kafischnaps* (just what it sounds like—coffee with *Schnaps*). In French-speaking Switzerland, the new bovine mums also get a taste of the farmer's preferred tipple—a bottle of good wine. As Robi said, they've earned it.

Alpabzug/Désalpe

The *Alpabzug/Désalpe* describes the tradition of farmers bringing their cows, which have spent the summer in higher Alpine pastures, back down to the valleys for the winter (in English this is called transhumance). The farmers decorate their herds with beautiful flower garlands and the cows wear their finest bells. The long walk down from the mountain pastures begins in the wee hours of the morning and they can be walking for four to six hours before they reach their farms.

In many regions there are festivals to welcome the cows home. There's typically a parade through town as well as alphorn music and yodeling, a market with local products (especially locally produced cheese) and a general celebration of Swiss farming life. You can hear the sound of the cowbells long before you see the cows, and by the time the herd is in front of you, the reverberations are rattling through your chest.

* Arguably more important than the *Röstigraben* (the invisible barrier between German and French-speaking Switzerland), this is this line that divides Switzerland's cow distribution and cultural life (meaning what kinds of cards they use to play Jass, Switzerland's favorite card game).

Alpabzug in Sumiswald, canton Bern

Delivery Dogs

Every morning, Swiss farmers fill metal tanks or cans with their milk and transport it to local dairies. On the way to school in our small Emmental town, my daughter often spots trails of milk along the roads and waves to the farmers in their Subarus or tractors.

A hundred years ago, they had animals to pull the carts—horses, donkeys, oxen, or even dogs. Farmers in canton Bern had their *Bäri*, a common name for the beautiful black, white and tan Bernese Mountain Dogs that come from the region. The dogs knew the way to the dairy, and would pull a little wagon laden with milk cans all by themselves to the dairy and then back home.

The Queen and the Milk Pipeline

The Val d'Hérens in the French-speaking part of canton Valais is full of idyllic Alpine trails, crystal blue lakes, craggy mountains, and charming chalets. It's also home to a queen. She has long lashes, silky black hair, and some of the most beautiful (and powerful) horns you have ever laid eyes on.

The cows of Hérens lock horns instinctively to establish a hierarchy, and the most powerful is the queen of the herd. In the Valais it's also a tradition for the strongest cows in each herd to fight each other as a spectator sport, resulting in the *Reine des Reines*, the Queen of Queens. The first winner, in 1923, was a cow named Violette, and a hundred years later her name was Mélodie.

You can see the cows tussling in news reports from 1956, however, the story of that day was not about bovine royalty, but rather about the highest milk pipeline in Europe. Directly from the alp, the farmers poured their milk through a large white funnel, where it would race down nearly 2000 m/1.25 mi of pipeline to the dairy in St. Martin.

HONIGMILCH

Honigmilch (honey milk) is a kind of cure-all in parts of Switzerland. Plenty of benefits are listed in old domestic household books including better sleep, lower blood pressure, a cure for colds, or anxiety reduction. Whether or not it achieves those goals, it is the perfect warm, comforting drink for cold winter nights.

Honey varies greatly in color and flavor, depending on what the bees collect. In general, floral honey (*Blütenhonig/Miel de fleurs*) is lighter in color and comes from bees that gather pollen from flowers in the spring. Darker forest honey, (*Waldhonig/Miel de forêt*) is collected later in the summer and comes from bees that collect pollen from forest leaves and flowers that have been chewed by aphids.

250 ml/1 cup milk
1 tsp wildflower honey

Heat the milk over medium heat, being careful not to let it boil. Stir in the honey until it melts. Pour into a mug and add a sprinkle of cinnamon on top, or to really put you to sleep, a shot of whiskey.

MILK PUNCH

Equally milky, but much less wholesome, is milk punch: a creamy, boozy, eggnog-adjacent drink that is perfect for the holiday season. It's not Swiss, per se, but a perfect vehicle for creamy, delicious Swiss milk.

100 ml/½ cup milk
50 ml/¼ cup brandy
30 ml/2 tbsp vanilla syrup
Ice
Fresh nutmeg

Place the milk, brandy, syrup and ice in a cocktail shaker and shake well. Pour into a glass and grate nutmeg over the top.

Ovomaltine

In the middle of the 1800s, one in five children in Switzerland died of malnutrition. Wanting to combat this problem, pharmacist and chemist Georg Wander, and later his son, Albert, experimented with malt in their Bernese laboratory. Eventually they succeeded in making a mix-in-milk powder using malt, egg, and milk, and flavored with cocoa: Ovomaltine. Wander was already an established company, producing a potpourri of pharmaceuticals and potions. Initially only available in pharmacies, by 1922 Ovomaltine had become Wander's flagship product and the company touted it as a drink for any time of day, from breakfast to before bed.

In 1937, Switzerland's war commission charged Wander with developing a version that the troops could take with them, and that could replace a meal—this became Ovo Sport. During the Second World War, drinking Ovomaltine was seen as an act of national solidarity, as well as an important source of nutrition for children. Today, the Swiss supply is still produced in the original factory in Neuenegg, near Bern, and the original recipe remains largely unchanged.

Swiss advertisements throughout the decades have consistently shown Ovomaltine, combined with Alpine milk and outdoor activities, to be the key to good health. Their famous tongue-in-cheek slogan *Mit Ovo chaschs nid besser. Aber länger!* (With Ovo you can't do it better. But longer!) spawned dozens of print and TV ads.

The first export of Ovomaltine was to Italy in 1906, and Britain soon followed in 1909. With factories all over the world, Ovo is appreciated by an international clientele to this day, and drunk by millions of people in over 100 countries worldwide.

(And no, English speakers, that's not a spelling mistake—the original name of the product was misspelled on its British trademark registration, leading to its English name of Ovaltine.)

The traditional preparation is simply to add Ovomaltine powder to warm milk and stir—though you can also serve it cold, and if you order it in a restaurant you will have to specify if you'd like it *kalt* or *heiss, froid* or *chaud.*

There are, however, many further uses of this wonderfully malty powder, and it's included in many drinks and baked goods recipes. In Switzerland, no sugar is added to the original Ovo blend, but in other countries it tends to be a bit sweeter, so bear that in mind when using it.

MALT ON MALT FLOAT

250 ml/1 cup dark beer
1 tbsp Ovomaltine powder
1 big scoop of vanilla ice cream

In a large beer glass, mix together the beer and Ovomaltine powder, then top with vanilla ice cream.

Stout, porter, *Schwarzbier*, or other dark beers work well—my favorite is *Schwarzer Kristall* made by Appenzeller Bier.

OVO FRAPPÉ

2 scoops vanilla ice cream
2 tbsp Ovomaltine powder
250 ml/1 cup milk

Blend well and garnish with Ovomaltine powder.

Famous Ovo drinkers

Sir Edmund Hillary purportedly took Ovo with him on his ascent of Mount Everest. Muhammad Ali swore by Ovaltine and there are fantastic photos of him promoting the drink during a whistle-stop tour of Great Britain in 1971.

Frappés

In Switzerland many restaurants don't have a typical dessert menu, but rather an ice cream menu. Ask for it and you'll get a little booklet with various *Coupes* (sundaes). Typically, there will be *Coupe Dänemark* (vanilla ice cream with self-serve warm chocolate sauce), *Sorbet Colonel* (lemon sorbet with vodka), definitely some variation of *Eiskaffee/Cafe Glacé* (mocha ice cream with whipped cream), hollow plastic 80s cartoon heads filled with ice cream for the kids (like Pingu, Smurfs, Tom and Jerry), and finally, the *frappés*.

Here, *frappés* are milkshakes, often topped with whipped cream and available in vanilla, chocolate and strawberry (though you'll occasionally find more adventurous flavors like lemon or hazelnut). In lots of other countries, especially Greece, a *frappé* involves coffee (and actually Swiss conglomerate Nestlé claims to have invented the Greek *frappé* at a trade fair in Thessaloniki—their trade rep couldn't find hot water so mixed Nescafé, water and ice in the chocolate milk shaker they had been demonstrating and voilà) but in Switzerland even a mocha version is entirely a milkshake.

Here are some variations, but they are extremely adaptable and you can use whatever ice cream flavors you have on hand. For best results, mix using a traditional or immersion blender.

Each recipe is for one *frappé*. Garnish with whipped cream as desired. In my house, a scoop of ice cream is around 50 g/¼ cup.

COUPE DÄNEMARK FRAPPÉ

2 scoops vanilla ice cream
200ml/¾ cup milk
Around 50 g/¼ cup chocolate sauce

Blend the ice cream and milk. Top with chocolate sauce.

CHERRY FRAPPÉ

2 scoops vanilla ice cream
2 tbsp cherry syrup
200 ml/¾ cup milk

Blend well and garnish with cherries. For a spirited addition, add a shot of *Rosoli* or *Röteli* (see pages 98 and 100).

SCHOGGI FRAPPÉ

2 scoops chocolate ice cream
50 g/¼ cup chocolate sauce
200 ml/¾ cup milk

Blend well and top with chopped chocolate.

CHOCOLATE SAUCE

100 g/½ cup chocolate
200 ml/¾ cup cream
Pinch of salt

Chop the chocolate and put it in a medium bowl.

Warm the cream over medium heat (keep an eye on this, as cream boils over very quickly).

Once the cream comes to a boil, pour it over the chocolate but do not stir.

Cover the bowl and let it sit for at least five minutes.

Add the salt and whisk the mixture until it's a glossy sauce.

Chapter 3: From Beans to Cups

Neither coffee nor cocoa comes from Switzerland, but you can't deny the impact that Swiss innovation has had on both products.

Coffee

It's difficult to believe that tiny Switzerland is a hub for the world's coffee supply. Incredibly, Switzerland exports more coffee than chocolate or cheese, and has been in the top-five coffee exporters in the world since 2009. The Swiss themselves love their brew and consistently rank in the top-10 coffee-drinking nations, too.

Chocolate

In the late 1800s Switzerland revolutionized chocolate production in two ways: in 1875 Daniel Peter made milk chocolate using powdered milk, and in 1879 Rodolphe Lindt invented the conching process, which pressed the gritty chocolate of the time into the smooth mass we know today.

Today the chocolate industry in Switzerland is still booming, with the Swiss themselves consuming per capita the highest proportion of chocolate worldwide. According to Chocosuisse, the organization of Swiss chocolate producers, the average Swiss person ate 11 kg/24 lb of chocolate in 2022 (I surely did). And one of my favorite ways to consume Swiss chocolate is in drinkable form—you'll find plenty of hot chocolate recipes starting on page 48.

Nescafé

What do bachelors, boy scouts, housewives, mountaineers and shift workers have in common? They were the groups targeted in 1937 as potential customers for Nestlé's newest product: instant coffee.

Created by Max Morgenthaler as a way to preserve Brazil's overabundant coffee bean harvests, this soluble powdered coffee was an instant success. Along the way, it's been to the moon and Earth's highest summit, and it was an essential ration for soldiers during the Second World War. Though it's probably not the drink of choice for real coffee lovers, Nescafé is sold in nearly every country in the world and remains popular to this day.

Coffee Business

By 1976, Nestlé engineer Eric Favre had already invented the Nespresso capsule system. Although it took almost three decades, Nespresso now dominates home coffee brewing. Available in 81 countries worldwide, all the coffee in Nespresso capsules is roasted and ground exclusively in Switzerland.

Nestlé wasn't the only player on the coffee scene. In 1851, the Volkart brothers from Winterthur became importers of spices, cotton, and coffee from India—and for much of the 20th century they were one of the largest coffee traders in the world.

Switzerland is also home to Eugster/Frismag, one of the world's largest producers of coffee machines under such brands as Jura, Turmix, and Koenig.

Ordering Coffee

When it comes to coffee at a restaurant or cafe anywhere in Switzerland, there's your typical array of Italian coffees—espresso, cappuccino, latte macchiato.

In German-speaking Switzerland, a *Café Crème* comes with a little pot of cream on the side, while a *Schale* is coffee with warm milk added.

If you want a milky coffee in French-speaking Switzerland, order a *renversé*, which means "reverse" and is so-named because you add the coffee to the milk and not vice versa.

Kaffeerahmdeckeli

It's the 1990s in a Swiss cafe. A group orders a round of coffee. The cups arrive at the table, and all eyes are on the thin aluminum lids on the little pots of cream sitting on each saucer.

Starting in 1968, the lids of coffee creamers in Switzerland, known as *Kaffeerahmdeckeli*, were printed with different motifs—every conceivable topic from Alpine flowers, dinosaurs, famous monks, and dog breeds, to blimps, bread, babies, Bratwurst and Bud Spencer. Since then, people have been collecting them, and the 1990s were the height of the boom.

Back to the cafe. People gently pull off the lids. Some pour the cream into their coffee, while others completely ignore it and drink their coffee black. They examine the lids, licking the backs, or wiping them on a napkin. They trade with each other. They tuck them into their purse or wallet. Kids from nearby tables approach cautiously, and brave ones inquire, "Do you have any extras? Any doubles?"

Children and grown-ups alike filled binders with the lids, many neatly arranged and labeled. I collected the cast-off lids from my mother and placed them in an envelope. I still have my collection—in fact many people do (just ask my in-laws, cousins, or next-door neighbor) and you can find numerous individual lids or entire binders for sale online.

If you weren't a collector and you made a motion to leave your table at a cafe or restaurant, the children and grown-ups might descend, trying to be the first to collect your discarded lid, trying to find a missing piece for their collection. It got so bad for some that they would deliberately put holes in the lids to prevent the collectors from crowding around their tables and adding to their treasures.

Milchkaffee

Enjoyed throughout the country, on farms, in villages, and cities, milky coffee is served not only for breakfast, but as an integral part of *Café Complet*, a simple dinner of bread, cheese, and cold cuts. My grandmother, like many Swiss, made *Milchkaffee* twice a day for much of her life. She'd fill two ceramic jugs, one with steamed milk and the other with her special coffee blend (a mixture of coffee and chicory, sometimes sweetened, sometimes not), to drink from little bowls called *Chacheli*. Due to the strength of the coffee, at least half of the cup would be filled with milk.

As coffee was traditionally an expensive product, most people could not afford to drink it pure. Many kinds of cheaper plants and grains were roasted and added to coffee—or, during very lean times, they replaced coffee entirely.

One of these plants was chicory, which has been produced as a coffee substitute in Switzerland since at least the early 1800s. After the Second World War, it became easier to get coffee, but many producers still added chicory for its subtle flavor and rich black color. Many Swiss, including my grandmother and mother-in-law, recognize it as an integral part of their morning brew.

To make your own *Milchkaffee*, use a mix of ground coffee and chicory—or you can buy pre-mixed chicory coffee in most Swiss supermarkets. My mother-in-law, Josy, gave me these tips: keep the water just under the boiling point to prevent the coffee from getting bitter, the milk should also not boil, and once you're done with the coffee grounds, add them to your garden—they make excellent fertilizer.

MILCHKAFFEE (Serves 8-10)

150–200 g/5–7 oz ground coffee
1 tbsp chicory
1 liter/4 cups water
1 liter/4 cups milk

Stovetop method: In a pot, heat the water and coffee to just below boiling. Remove from the heat, leave the grounds to settle, then ladle or pour the coffee into a jug.

Pour over method: Add the coffee to a coffee filter placed over a large jug. Heat the water in a kettle and just before it boils, gradually pour it through the filter.

Warm, but don't boil, the milk. Add to a jug and serve immediately. A skin tends to form on the hot milk, so use a sieve when pouring. The typical ratio of milk to coffee is at least 1:1.

A Coffee Fix in Many Forms

The Swiss are coffee lovers first and foremost. Here are some other applications of coffee—whipped, cold, and sweet.

WHIPPED COFFEE

One of the viral sensations that took over the world during the first COVID-19 pandemic lockdown was Dalgona, or whipped coffee; something that was only possible because of a Swiss invention—Nescafé instant coffee.

Attributed to a shipbuilder in Macau who first made the drink in 1997, this technique of beating instant coffee, hot water and sugar into a gloriously frothy and creamy coffee has been popularized around the world.

2 tbsp instant coffee powder
2 tbsp sugar
2 tbsp boiling water
Ice
Milk of choice

Place the coffee powder, sugar and water in a large measuring cup. Using a hand mixer with a whisk attachment, beat until frothy. Spoon over milk and ice.

COLD BREW

Cold brew is a cold infused coffee, no heating required, as opposed to iced coffee, which is usually just hot coffee poured over ice. It's usually pretty strong—when tempered with milk, it's delightful, and when tempered with vanilla ice cream, it's heavenly.

200 g/7 oz coffee, coarsely ground
2 liters/8 cups cold water

Pour the cold water into a container, add the ground coffee and whisk well.

Cover, and let sit overnight.

In the morning, strain into containers using a sieve and a coffee filter (this can take quite a while), then funnel into bottles. Keep in the fridge and drink within a few days.

COFFEE SYRUP

If you have cold brew, it's very easy to make coffee syrup, which is great to drizzle over ice cream or mix with cold milk. Simply combine equal parts coffee and sugar, cook over medium heat until the sugar has dissolved, strain and bottle. Keep in the fridge and use within a week or so.

Kafischnaps

Let's talk about the real reason many Swiss attend cold outdoor events: *Kafischnaps* (exactly what it sounds like, coffee laced with *Schnaps*).

It has a light coffee base (often instant), a good splash of spirits and a cube of sugar. One method has you toss a *Füüfliber* (5-franc coin) into a glass, fill it up with coffee until you can't see it anymore, then add the *Schnaps* until you can see it again. The coffee is, typically, extremely weak and looks more like tea—some recipes call for the sugar, booze and a *Prise* (pinch), or simply *ein paar Körnchen* (a couple granules), of instant coffee at the bottom of the glass before filling it up with hot water.

Boozy coffee is drunk all over the country—in restaurants and cafes, at events and at home—with small variations in name and preparation from place to place. In German-speaking Switzerland you will hear it called by different names, like *Kafi Fertig*, and *Kafi Luz* or *Lutz*. *Kafi Träsch* means it's spiked with the spirit of the same name, and the same goes for *Chrüter*, which adds herbal spirits, and *Halb-Halb*, a *Schnaps* that is half plum, half apple and pear. *Kafi GT* just means that cream is added, and a *Cheli* indicates your drink will be served in a *Chacheli* (a small bowl).

The coffee is better, but the spirits are similar: in French-speaking Switzerland you can request your desired intoxicant, like *café kirsch* or *café prune*, whereas asking for *caffè coretto* or *caffè grappa* in Ticino will get you a tipple in your brew.

Äntlibuecher Kafi

The people of the Entlebuch, in the central Swiss canton of Lucerne, are great consumers and possible originators of *Kafischnaps*; theirs is known as *Äntlibuecher Kafi*.

My friend Friedrich, born and raised in the heart of the region, declares it as much a part of his homeland as the landscape. He gives the history as follows: as soon as coffee drinking had been established in the city, the rural folk took up the habit and adapted it to their liking. This meant brewing weaker coffee (saving on expensive beans) and adding booze (personal preference). Although the moral authorities of the time criticized what they considered their lavishness, this didn't stop the Entlebuchers.

Local farmers were sneaky in finding excuses for distilling extra alcohol. Until 2013 every farm had the right to distill some of its own alcohol, tax-free. The amount was based on the size of the farm and the number of animals—this could be upwards of 45 liters/12 gallons of pure alcohol, per year. Friedrich assures me that not all bottles were consumed for official purposes and plenty made it into *Äntlibuecher Kafi* instead.

Not only did Friedrich give me the lowdown on *Äntlibuecher Kafi*, he also gave me his recipe; though he made it clear that more important than the recipe itself is the environment when brewing and drinking. The ideal conditions would be a hut in a forest, with a wood-fired stove and a bunch of good friends. The drink should contain so much booze that it's transparent—you should be able to read a newspaper through the glass.

ÄNTLIBUECHER KAFI (Serves 5)

1 liter/4 cups water
1 small handful instant coffee (about a tablespoon)
1 fir branch
Schnaps of choice (eg. Träsch, Zwetschgen, Williams, kirsch, Halb-Halb)
Sugar cubes

Bring the water to a boil. Put the coffee in the water and stir with a fir branch.

Drop the fir branch in, let it boil for one minute, then discard. Let the covered pan rest until all the coffee has dissolved.

Lighten it up with *Schnaps*, by adding about one ladle full. Pour it into a coffee glass and add a sugar cube (or two).

Hot Chocolate

The Swiss drink their chocolate in many forms.

At my grandmother's breakfast table, my cousins and I always drank *Schüttelmilch*, shaken milk, which was simply chocolate powder in cold milk, shaken until foamy. You can even buy special colorful cups, with screw-on lids, made just for this. In the winter, the kids would sometimes steal a bit of milk from the grown-ups' *Milchkaffee*, and have a warm chocolate milk for breakfast.

Out and about, at restaurants and cafes, the kind of drinking chocolate varies wildly. In big self-service restaurants like the ones at many ski resorts, you might get it out of a machine, hot, foamy, and very sweet. If it's served to you, you will likely find yourself with a mug of warm, frothed milk, and a little packet of Caotina or Suchard chocolate powder that you have to stir in yourself. I'm always on the lookout for a version made in-house—with real chocolate—rich, creamy, and not too sweet.

At home, of course, you have the opportunity to fine tune your hot chocolate to your liking. Cocoa powder? Milk or dark chocolate? Just milk, or a splash of cream?

A good hot chocolate can be rich and thick, almost tempting you to eat it with a spoon, or it can be slightly lighter, allowing you to drink it fast and warm up quickly. The best chocolate drinks demand the best (Swiss) chocolate or cocoa powder you can find.

Here, I have a few different recipes—Big Batch Cocoa and Dreamy, Creamy Hot Chocolate, and even a quick one-mug version. All recipes make one serving, except Big Batch Cocoa which serves 10.

COCOA

200 ml/¾ cup milk
1 tbsp unsweetened cocoa powder
2 tsp sugar
Drizzle of vanilla paste or extract
Pinch of salt

Whisk everything together in a small pot. Warm over medium heat, but don't boil.

BIG BATCH COCOA (Serves 10)

2 liters/8 cups milk
200 g/1 cup sugar
2 tbsp vanilla paste or extract
1 tsp salt
150 g/1¼ cup unsweetened cocoa
* powder*

Whisk together the milk, sugar, vanilla and salt in a large pot. Sift in the cocoa powder and whisk well. Warm over medium heat, but don't boil.

DREAMY, CREAMY HOT CHOCOLATE

200 ml/¾ cup milk
30 g/1 oz dark chocolate, chopped
20 g/0.7 oz milk chocolate,
* chopped*
Pinch of salt
50 ml/¼ cup cream

Over medium heat, warm the milk in a pot until simmering.

In the microwave or in a bowl over simmering water, melt the chocolate.

Whisk the chocolate and salt into the warm milk, then whisk in the cream.

Warm to desired temperature.

(You don't *have* to melt the chocolate separately, but it does make for an impossibly smooth drink. Alternatively, you can just add the chopped chocolate to the warmed milk and whisk well.)

DECADENT DARK HOT CHOCOLATE

200 ml/¾ cup milk
2 tsp cocoa powder
30 g/1 oz dark chocolate, chopped
Pinch of salt

Heat the milk until simmering, whisk in the cocoa powder, then the dark chocolate and salt.

QUICK HOT CHOCOLATE

Place three red Lindor truffles in a mug. Add 200 ml/¾ cup hot milk and stir until the balls are dissolved.

Chapter 4: From the Breweries

Beer on Tap

The most commonly ordered beer in German-speaking Switzerland is the *Stange*. This is not a kind of beer, but rather the glass—tall and straight and resembling its name, *Stange* (bar or rod). It holds around 300 ml/10 fl oz and will typically be filled with standard lager. In some places, when this amount is served in a round glass, it's called a *Chübeli* or *Rugeli*.

In German-speaking Switzerland, ordering a Grosses, or a *Chöbu/Kübel*, will get you half a liter/17 fl oz and, although rarer in Switzerland, you might see a whole liter called a *Mass*, *Litron* or *Krug*. A smaller beer clocks in at 200 ml/7 fl oz and is sometimes referred to as a *Herrgöttli*. This was a nickname of Lucerne's infamous and charismatic art and church supply dealer Anton Achermann. Notoriously frugal, he preferred a smaller, less expensive beer, and soon his nickname was associated with the glass.

In French-speaking Switzerland, order a beer by asking for a *binch* or a *pression*.

If you're looking for something a little lighter, order a *Panaché*. Like the German *Radler* or British Shandy, it's a mix of beer and pop—in this case 7UP, Sprite, or Swiss Elmer Citro.

Monastery Microbrew

It was monastery dwellers who developed a rich brewing tradition in medieval Europe, including those at the Abbey of St. Gallen.

Today, its library is a treasure trove of medieval rarities. This includes the ninth-century Plan of Saint Gall, the only existing architectural plan from the Middle Ages, which included three large, detailed brewhouses. Although it was never actually built, it's interpreted as an example of an ideal monastic complex, and one where beer brewing played a central role in the nourishment of the monks.

GLÜHBIER (Serves 2)

Reminiscent of *Glühwein*, this dark and citrusy brew is the perfect winter warmer.

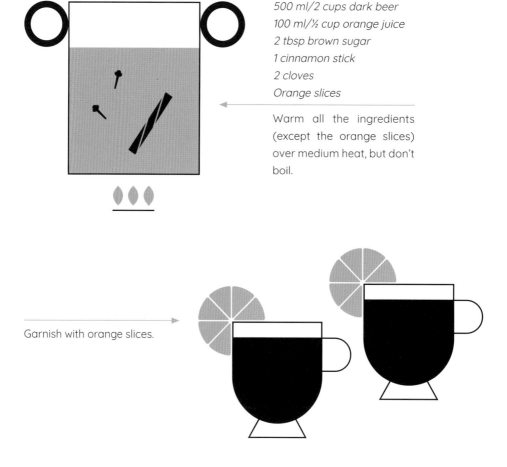

500 ml/2 cups dark beer
100 ml/½ cup orange juice
2 tbsp brown sugar
1 cinnamon stick
2 cloves
Orange slices

Warm all the ingredients (except the orange slices) over medium heat, but don't boil.

Garnish with orange slices.

The Reign of the Swiss Beer Cartel

In 1890 there were about 500 domestic breweries in Switzerland, but by 1998 this had dwindled to 24. What happened?

An association of brewers, the *Schweizerischer Bierbrauerverein*, was founded in 1887. After the financial collapse following the First World War, the association lobbied successfully to impose high taxes on imported beers. By 1935 they had enough control of the market to write their own convention. The organization worked as a cartel, controlling everything from beer distribution to the size of bottles and ingredients used. Restaurants, hotels, shops, and supermarkets were forced into exclusive contracts.

What was initially seen as a protection of Swiss beer, eventually became its undoing. With no reason to change and no competition, innovation suffered, and so did the beer. Finally, in the 1990s, the cartel collapsed and foreign beers flooded the market, providing consumers with a better choice and product. Ironically, almost all of the cartel breweries were bought by foreign companies like Heineken and Carlsberg—the very thing they had tried to avoid less than a century before.

Swiss Craft Beer

At their weakest, the breweries may have numbered 24, but the rebuilding of the Swiss beer market, in tandem with a worldwide surge in craft beer sales in the early 2000s, has meant a growth of microbreweries. According to the Swiss register of brewers, there are over 1000 active breweries registered in Switzerland today, the highest number of breweries per capita in the world.

Although the big breweries of the past still seem to dominate, Swiss craft beer is a small but thriving scene. Located in seemingly every *Scheune* and *Spycher* (barn and storehouse) in the country, there is a local brewery near you that is worth exploring.

There are far too many great brewers to mention, though the one exception is *Brasserie des Franches Montagnes*, or BFM, the grandfather of craft beer in Switzerland. After completing a degree in viticulture, Jérôme Rebetez founded the brewery in his home canton, Jura, in 1997. Brewed using traditional cask methods, as well as occasional unconventional ingredients (lapsang souchong tea, Sarawak peppers, gummy bears), the beers of BFM have received international acclaim. In 2009, their *L'Abbaye de Saint Bon-Chien* was voted the best beer in the world by *The New York Times*.

Monstein

Sebastian "Basti" Degen is a busy man. The Franconian import with the big smile and booming voice has a wave and a word for most of the locals in Monstein, Graubünden, the tiny Swiss town he calls home. And why not? He's the man in charge of one of their most famous landmarks, the brewery.

Picture this: it's 2000 and a lawyer, a graphic designer, a contractor and a hotelier all walk into a bar. Later, they walk out with the idea for Monstein, and out of the town's former and derelict Alpine dairy they build the brewery, which opens the following year. This *Schnapsidee* (an idea you have while drinking) grows, and the brewery flourishes. Today Monstein is one of the 80 biggest breweries in Switzerland—remarkable for a company that doesn't send much beer outside of the canton. Typically their beers stay within an 80 km/50 mi radius of the brewery.

Basti first came to Switzerland as a young brewer in 2007, and despite a few years dabbling abroad, eventually ended up back in Monstein not only as their *Braumeister* (head brewer) but also as their general manager.

We sit opposite the brewery in a hotel bar, one that proudly serves Monstein beer. Sipping his coffee and chatting casually with both the hotel staff and his own, Basti tells me the story of the company. During all this he also manages to take calls, in-between writing an order for three crates of beer on the back of a coaster. It's clear that he's the beating heart of the brewery, which for all its success and dominance in the region, is still quite a small company—they have three brewers, someone to do the office work, and two to three helpers.

Their product range includes many traditional styles—amber, lager, *Weizen*, *Märzen*—as well as specialty, seasonal and non-alcoholic beers. You can visit the brewery, too. On Fridays you can stop by for an informal drink and chat with the staff. You might even get to drink beer from the life-sized, wood-carved mountain goat with a built-in Monstein tap.

For Basti, he's living the dream—he knew at 10 years old that he wanted to be a brewer, though "that can be hard on your parents," he says with a smile.

"What's your favorite beer?" I ask him.

"Free beer," he says, and flashes a big grin.

Top right, Basti Degen

Chapter 5: From the Vines

One of Switzerland's best kept secrets is its excellent wine. Per capita, the Swiss drink about 40 bottles per person per year, according to the Federal Office of Agriculture, which puts them in the top 10 wine-consuming nations worldwide. However, only a teensy 1–2% is exported.

The two most popular grape varieties in Switzerland are Pinot Noir, which makes light, peppery red wines, and Chasselas (known as Fendant in Valais), a light crisp white that pairs perfectly with—you guessed it—cheese. Switzerland also has some endemic grapes, and some that may have origins elsewhere but are grown pretty much exclusively here.

These varieties below are worth seeking out.

Whites
- **Amigne** is a historic white wine grape from the Valais, which was likely introduced by the Romans. The grapes produce white wines that are citrusy and light, with a nice sweetness.
- In Graubünden don't miss **Completer**, an Alpine grape which dates from 1321 and makes rich, strong whites, full of character.
- **Heida** is often referred to as the pearl of Alpine wine and grown at high altitudes, like the St. Jodern Kellerei, with vineyards at 1150 m/3770 ft. It is a full-bodied wine that retains a nice freshness.
- Two very rare grapes currently making a comeback are **Himbertscha** and **Lafnetscha**, which produce wild and unpredictable Valais wines.
- Thought to be high in iron and once given to mothers who had just given birth, **Humagne Blanc** is an ancient grape variety that produces another citrusy, easy drinking Valais white wine.
- **Petite Arvine** is an old grape variety unique to the Valais that has been traced back to 1602. It produces the best-regarded white wine from the region: fruity with little bitterness and a light citrusy taste.

Reds

- **Cornalin** is a sensitive red grape from Valais that requires a great deal of attention. In the mid-20th century it almost disappeared from production; but, recently resurrected, it now stands as the centerpiece of the Valais red wines. This is a fruity, bright red wine that mellows with age.
- **Dôle** is a blended wine made from 85% Pinot Noir and Gamay grapes. The rest is a mix of other Valais grapes, such as Syrah, Humagne Rouge, or Cornalin, which add additional structure, color and flavor. It varies greatly, depending on the terroir and vintner, but is usually a fine, aromatic red wine.
- **Humagne Rouge** is an offspring of Cornalin and produces a wild and rustic wine. Drunk young, it retains a nice fruitiness, but it can be cellared for three to five years for maximum flavor.

Municipal Wine Collections

Many towns and cities in Switzerland have municipal vineyards. They are owned by the local government and the wine can be used for community events, given as gifts, or sold to the public.

Some of these vineyards have belonged to their municipalities for centuries. The ones belonging to the city of Bern, with their prime location on the lake of Biel, are actually the biggest series of vineyards in the whole canton. Though once owned by local monasteries, they have belonged to the city of Bern, the *Einwohnergemeinde*, since 1833. The city of Zurich has a large vineyard overseen by notable vintner Karin Schär, and the city of Schaffhausen's grapes grow on the side of the Munot, the famous round fortification overlooking the city. The resulting wine is affectionately called the *Munötler*.

But it isn't just big cities—in the French-speaking, wine-producing regions of western Switzerland, even the smallest towns have their own vineyards. There, it isn't just about the practical benefit of making your own wine, but also a celebration of the long-standing tradition of winemaking in the region, and the quality of the *Vin de Commune* from towns like Aigle or Lutry can be phenomenal.

The Highest Vineyard in Europe

The idea of a collective wine supply is hardly recent, as small plots of vineyards have been pooling their resources for centuries.

Take, for example, the families who own the purportedly highest vineyard in Europe at Visperterminen in Valais. Different owners maintain various parts (and sizes) of these historic vines, which sit as high as 1150 m/3770 ft above sea level. They typically pick the grapes themselves, by hand, as the height and slope prevent mechanized harvesting.

The grapes are processed and sold by the cooperative St. Jodern Kellerei, an association set up and overseen by the families. The pearl of the wines they produce is Heida, which thrives under the sun in high altitudes.

The World's Smallest Vineyard

High in the Alps of Valais, the smallest vineyard in the world is made up of three vines and named after a famous counterfeiter. *La vigne à Farinet* (Farinet's vineyard) is only 1.618 m², slightly larger than a queen-sized bed. Its name serves as a tribute to the man dubbed the Robin Hood of the Alps.

Born in Aosta, Italy, in 1845, Joseph-Samuel Farinet was a lively drinker and womanizer who made his fortune counterfeiting money. On the run from Italian authorities, he hid among the peasants of the Valais and continued his crimes, forging 20-centime pieces. But he was also a generous rogue who shared his counterfeit money with the locals, lifting them out of debt and improving their lives. They mourned him in 1880 when his body was found in a gorge near Saillon, and today he remains a symbol of the wild heart of the region.

It was Jean-Louis Barrault, a French actor who portrayed Farinet in a film from the 1930s, who founded the Friends of Farinet and conceived of the tiny vineyard as a place for people to retreat from the stresses of modern life. He eventually gave the vineyard to Abbé Pierre, a Catholic priest famed for fighting in the French Resistance and founding the charity Emmaus, who in turn gave the property to the Dalai Lama in 1999.

Each year, notable people work the land—from Jane Birkin and Claudia Cardinale to Michael Schumacher and Roger Moore. All the bottles produced (1000 per year; supplemented heavily with grapes from nearby vineyards) are sold to raise money for charity.

Top, Chateau d'Aigle; bottom, Terrasses de Lavaux; both in canton Vaud

The Most Beautiful Swiss Vineyards

The stunning *Terrasses de Lavaux* along Lake Geneva are not only beautiful, but they are also the largest area of adjoining vineyards in the country. Rising up along the steep incline from the lake, they extend 30 km/19 mi, from Vevey to Lausanne.

The area has always favored grape growing, especially Chasselas, and its traceable history goes back to 12th-century monasteries. Since 2007 the terraces have been listed as a UNESCO World Heritage Site, with the organization calling it: "an outstanding example of a centuries-long interaction between people and their environment." Today the region is popular for hikers and wine-lovers alike, and there are plenty of opportunities to taste the wine as you go.

BOTTOMS UP!

Switzerland has numerous wine museums, and here are some favorites:

- Vinorama in Ermatigen, canton Thurgau, puts wine in a historic context and features a look back at life in the region in the 1900s.
- In the middle of Switzerland's most prolific winegrowing canton, the wine museum in Salgesch, Valais, features many interactive activities like wine tasting and meeting local winegrowers.
- The Weinkrone in Hallau, Schaffhausen, is a lovely little museum with a cute bistro for wine tastings.
- You can learn about the history of wine in the stunning Chateau d'Aigle, Vaud, an imposing castle surrounded by vineyards and well worth the trip.

The Oldest Swiss Wine

Vin des Glaciers
High in the mountains of Valais you will find the *Vin des Glaciers*, wine in barrels that are never emptied.

Since at least the 18th century, Alpine dwellers have been filling their larch barrels with each year's wine, then cellaring them in nearby mountain villages. Also called "the sherry of Valais," today some drops of this golden liquid are over 125 years old.

The wine isn't sold; rather, it's drunk by the vintners on occasions that warrant it, such as births, weddings and funerals. Occasionally, a few lucky outsiders are able to taste the wine in the small town of Grimentz in the Val d'Anniviers.

The Youngest Swiss Wine

Sauser/Vin Bourru
I've made the common mistake with *Sauser*. Despite my husband reminding me not to tip the bottle, it found its way onto its side and sploosh, all our groceries were covered in grape juice.

Sauser is a fermented, slightly sparkling, freshly pressed grape juice that is available to buy during the grape harvest. When you buy it, it contains about 4% alcohol, which increases the longer it sits in your fridge, topping out at about 10%. Because this young wine has begun its fermentation process, gasses are constantly escaping from the bottle. To allow these to escape without the bottle exploding, they have thin aluminum tops with air holes.

Wine That Isn't Wine At All

Rimuss
In Switzerland, if you want to "cheers" with your children on New Year's Eve, or pop open a bottle of something bubbly on their birthdays, you'll probably pour them a flute of the alcohol-free grape juice Rimuss. Originating in the winegrowing village of Hallau, in canton Schaffhausen, this classic fizzy drink has been delighting kids and nondrinkers since the 1950s.

Grimentz in canton Valais

Oeil-de-Perdrix

Oeil-de-Perdrix (eye of the partridge) is a rosé wine that is a specialty of Neuchâtel.

It originated in France in the Middle Ages. Vintners tried to deepen the flavor of their white wine in an attempt to compete with the popular Burgundies of the time, so they used red grapes to make their whites. The Neuchâteloise version is made from Pinot Noir grapes. The pale rosy color remains and gives the wine its name, as it is said to be the color of the eye of a dying partridge.

Later on, winemakers perfected the process of colorlessly producing white wine from red grapes, but Oeil-de-Perdrix is made using the original methods and retains its glorious pale pink.

It was this wine that led to the most profound and polemic wine revolution in the United States—the rise of White Zinfandel. White Zinfandel is a sweet, pink wine that oenophiles love to hate. However, in the late 1980s it became the best-selling wine in America, and its creator was praised for introducing wine to more Americans than ever before.

So what does White Zin have to do with Oeil-de-Perdrix?

The winery in Northern California that would eventually produce the White Zinfandel was founded by Swiss immigrants at the end of the 19th century. After the Second World War, the winery was purchased by Italian brothers from New York, who eventually tried their hand at making an Oeil-de-Perdrix-style wine, using California's favorite red grape, Zinfandel.

A couple of years into their experimentation, one of their batches failed due to stuck fermentation (when the yeast dies before it has converted all of the sugars into alcohol), so the wine was put aside. Two weeks later they were pleased to discover that the sweet pink drink tasted delicious.

Although they attempted to call it Oeil-de-Perdrix, the Bureau of Alcohol, Tobacco and Firearms thought the name would be too confusing to the American public, so the vintners just named it after the grape, calling the pink wine White Zinfandel.

Ironically, although the wine snobs thought White Zin was an overly sweet, pedestrian wine, it was because of its popularity that many old Zinfandel vines were preserved and would later be used to create impressive red Zinfandels in the 1990s.

In general, Oeil-de-Perdrix is a balanced, dry wine, not sweet, and perfect for light summer foods and creamy sauces. You can happily drink it on its own, but it also makes nice cocktails, like this variation on a typical Bellini.

OEIL-DE-PERDRIX BELLINI

4 peaches
Water
1 tbsp sugar
1 bottle Oeil-de-Perdrix, chilled

First, make the peach purée.

Peel the peaches—you can do this one of two ways: with a vegetable peeler if they are firm enough, or dip the peaches in boiling water for about half a minute, then place in a bowl of cold water. Wait a few minutes and then pierce and remove the skin.

Cut the peaches into chunks, removing the stone.

Add a splash of water into a pot, so it just covers the bottom, then add the peaches and sugar. Cook over medium heat until the fruit has broken up, then blend thoroughly (an immersion or regular blender work best) and let cool completely.

Add a couple of tablespoons of the purée into four glasses, top with chilled Oeil-de-Perdrix, and stir.

Bowle

A *Bowle* is the German version of punch. It is extremely versatile: you can make it boozy or not, sweet or not too sweet, and use an array of seasonal fruits.

Susannah Müller, the pioneering Swiss nutritionist and writer, included numerous variations in her classic cooking and domestic-advice book from 1860 *Das fleissige Hausmütterchen* (The Industrious Little Housewife), including pineapple, apricot, peach, orange, and raspberry. Beloved Swiss school textbook *Tiptopf* has a recipe for a choose-your-own-fruit *Früchtebowle* with apple juice, and the timeless Swiss cookbook author Elisabeth Fülscher uses a bottle of champagne in one of her variations. *Cin cin!*

Here, I have recipes for strawberry and apricot versions, both of which use elderflower syrup (recipe on page 26). For the photos, I used lots of rose petals and elderflower blossoms, but actually it's not so pleasant to get a mouthful while drinking, so I would strain out the flowers when serving.

For a non-alcoholic version, replace the wine with of sparkling water (adding more elderflower syrup to taste), or omit the elderflower syrup altogether and replace the regular wine with a non-alcoholic wine, like Rimuss, or a not-too-sweet white grape juice.

STRAWBERRY BOWLE (Serves 6)

300 g/10 oz strawberries, sliced
50 ml/¼ cup elderflower syrup
Juice of 1 lemon
1 bunch mint, roughly chopped
1 bottle white or sparkling wine

Place the strawberries and mint in a large pitcher. Add the lemon juice and elderflower syrup and stir together. Let sit for about an hour. Top with wine and serve.

I like to start with about 50 ml/¼ cup of elderflower syrup, because you can always add more if you find it not quite sweet enough.

APRICOT BOWLE (Serves 12)

500 g/1 lb apricots, sliced
60 g/⅓ cup sugar
50 ml/¼ cup elderflower syrup
100 ml/½ cup Abricotine or other apricot brandy
Two bottles sparkling wine

In a punch bowl, toss the apricots with the sugar and let sit for about an hour. Stir in the syrup and brandy, then top with sparkling wine.

Depending on how sweet your wine is, you may need to add a little more or less sugar.

Hugo

Although it didn't originate here (it was founded just across the Italian border), Hugo is one of Switzerland's favorite summer drinks. Roland Gruber, a beardy, South Tyrolean vagabond barkeep, mixed together *Zitronenmelissensirup* (lemon balm syrup), Prosecco, mint, and a spritz of soda water, thought up a name off the top of his head, and served it to regulars at his bar in Naturns in 2005.

Other than a bit of notoriety, Gruber didn't really get any compensation for creating what would become one of the most ubiquitous drinks in the German-speaking realm. By 2010 it had spread from Sylt to Schwyz and was a standard summer cocktail at bars, restaurants, and hotels.

The ingredients have changed slightly, with many bartenders preferring elderflower syrup or adding lime, and some replace the Prosecco with white wine or champagne.

Today it remains a refreshing classic on a warm summer's day (or any day for that matter).

HUGO

3–4 mint leaves
1–2 tbsp elderflower syrup
Prosecco/sparkling wine
Sparkling water
1 lime

Muddle the mint leaves, put them in a wine glass and cover with ice cubes. Add the elderflower syrup and top with prosecco/sparkling wine and a spritz of sparkling water. Stir and garnish with lime.

Gruber's original recipe uses 150 ml/⅔ cup of prosecco, then is topped with sparkling water, but you can alter this as you see fit. He also prefers lemon balm syrup, using 20 ml/4 tsp in his recipe.

Glühwein

My husband, Sam, looked skeptically at my *Glühwein* simmering on the stove, not a lemon in sight.

"That looks expensive," he said, picking up the empty wine bottle.
"Barely 12 francs!" I protested.

A long sigh. For Sam, who's used to making *Glühwein* (mulled wine) in stockpots on portable burners, ladling it out to glassy-eyed, rosy-faced friends, spending 12 Swiss francs is obscene.

But this isn't your typical Christmas market *Glühwein*. This is a generously spiced, served at an intimate dinner party kind of *Glühwein*. It's my replacement for eggnog at all kinds of Christmas events: from Christmas card writing to decorating the tree. It's how to be a festive wine mom. The citrus is in the garnish only, the spices are warm and festive, and it's just a little bit sweet.
Cheers, Sam.

ANDIE'S GLÜHWEIN (Serves 4)

3 each of cardamom pods,
  peppercorns, cloves
2 each of cinnamon sticks,
  slices of ginger
1 each of star anise, bay leaf
2–3 tbsp sugar or red wine syrup
  (recipe p. 25)
1 bottle red wine
Orange slices to garnish

Add the spices, sugar and wine to a large pot. Heat on medium, making sure it doesn't boil. If desired, garnish with orange slices.

Pick a wine you might like to drink on its own—not too expensive, mind you, because you are spicing and sweetening it, but not the cheapest either. I like to use a peppery Swiss Pinot Noir. Other fruity reds would also do the trick, like a Dôle.

SAM'S GLÜHWEIN (Serves 8)

Need mulled wine for a crowd? Here's my husband's go-to recipe. No 12-franc bottles of wine here!

4 black tea bags
1 cinnamon stick
3 cloves
2 bottles of cheap red wine
50–100 g/¼–½ cup sugar
Around 50 ml/¼ cup brandy or rum
3 each of oranges and lemons,
  sliced into rounds

In a large pot, place the tea bags and spices with about 400 ml/1⅔ cups of water. Bring to a boil, then remove the tea bags, add the red wine and turn down the temperature to low. Add the sugar, booze, and citrus slices, and keep at a low simmer. Before serving, remove the spices.

HYPOKRAS (Serves 8-10)

It's in Basel where *Hypokras* (festive spiced wine) is most beloved today—so much so that it pours from their *Dreizackbrunnen*, a famous fountain, on New Year's Day. With a glass in one hand and a *Basler Läckerli* in the other, it's the perfect way to start the year off right.

The book *Basler Kochschule* (Basel's cooking school) was first published in 1877 by Amalie Schneider-Schlöth and has a recipe for *Hypokras*. She suggests using an *erstklassiger* (first-class) white wine, and a Roussillon or good Bordeaux for the red. Meant to be made in advance and rested for two weeks, my scaled-down version serves 8–10 people.

1 bottle of dry white wine
100 g/½ cup sugar
2 each of cinnamon sticks and
  cloves
1 bottle of red wine

In a large pot over medium heat, cook the white wine, sugar and spices until all the sugar has dissolved. Remove from the heat, stir in the red wine and let cool. Strain into bottles, then let rest two weeks before serving.

VIN BLANC CHAUD (Serves 4)

I love serving this white mulled wine as an apéro to a fondue dinner—it's a great start to the white wine and warm tea that I continue to serve throughout the evening.

1 bottle of white wine
2 cinnamon sticks
3 star anise
2 oranges, in slices
2 lemons, in slices
50 g/¼ cup honey

Put everything in a pot and warm over medium heat, making sure it doesn't boil.

Before serving, have a quick taste—if it isn't sweet enough, add a tablespoon more honey, or a squeeze of orange juice (this will very much depend on the sweetness of the wine and your personal preference).

Grappa—When the Winemaking's Over

In winemaking, once the grapes have been pressed, the parts that remain are often themselves distilled. The leftover skins and seeds, called "pomace" in English, are distilled to make Marc. Or you might be more familiar with the Italian name—*grappa*.

Now protected throughout Europe, *grappa* can only be produced in Italy, the Swiss canton of Ticino, or San Marino. In Ticino, it's been made since at least the 1800s, especially in Santa Maria del Bigorio, a Capuchin monastery founded in 1535. Today it is beloved in the region and throughout the country. Often in Ticino it's made with a strain of *uva americana* (American grapes) that lend a notable "foxy" aroma to the spirit.

GRAPPA ALEXANDER

50 ml/1.7 fl oz grappa
50 ml/1.7 fl oz Crème de Cacao
50 ml/1.7 fl oz cream
Nutmeg to garnish

Shake with ice.

Strain into a glass.
Garnish with nutmeg.

Chapter 6: From the Orchards

Dotted around Swiss farms are always plenty of fruit (and nut) trees. In the spring, their white and pink blossoms herald the arriving warmer weather. But it isn't just about looks: these trees promote biodiversity (housing all kinds of birds and insects), prevent soil erosion and help absorb carbon dioxide.

The trees provide fruit to eat as well as to preserve and conserve for the colder months ahead. The nuts from the trees can be pressed into oil, while pears and apples are made into juice and cider. Some fruits are left to ferment in big vats and later distilled into different fruit brandies.

And what is Switzerland's favorite fruit?

Fittingly, the apple. According to the Swiss Farmers' Association, the Swiss eat 16 kg/35 lb of apples per year: more than any other fruit. Other popular fruits include pears, cherries, plums and, in the Valais, apricots.

Most

Freshly pressed apple (and pear) juice can be found all over Switzerland in the fall, from your local market to your local Migros. Although the fresh juice is particularly delicious, today much of the product is pasteurized, bottled, and available year-round.

Referred to as *Most* or *Moscht* in German-speaking Switzerland (*cidre* in French), the apple juice can be non-alcoholic, as in *Süssmost*, or alcoholic, as in *saurer*, *suure* or *Alte Most*. The name *Most* is from the Latin word for freshly pressed grapes, *vinum mustum*.

Saurer Most stems from at least the Middle Ages when farmers would make vinegar and lightly alcoholic drinks with their apple juice. Apple juice naturally ferments after a few days, so it wasn't until the early 1900s that pasteurization (which stops the fermentation and allows it to remain alcohol-free) made it possible for the non-alcoholic version to be stored and sold at market.

Süssmost then became popular with children and athletes—and the government, which was trying to combat alcoholism. In the 1920s, laborers drank up to 5–6 liters/10–12 pints of alcoholic *Most* per day—farmers drank 1 liter/2 pints before milking, and factory workers received a 2-liter/4-pint ration per shift, not to mention the shots of apple *Schnaps* that started the day. According to biologist and apple enthusiast Brigitte Bartha-Pichler, Switzerland produced and drank, at that time, the most *Schnaps* in all of Europe. Even during poor harvest years, much of Switzerland's fruit was being used to make alcoholic drinks, so the government offered subsidies and made legislation to encourage the production and consumption of the softer variety of juice.

Schorle

A variation on the theme is the *Schorle*—which just indicates that the juice is diluted with a bit of water, most often sparkling, though sometimes still. *Schorles* exist in as many variations as there are fruits, but apple is the most popular.

The Mostbummel

At one time, before pasteurization, *Süssmost* was a luxurious, yet fleeting, drink. Once the pressed juice began to ferment, the alcoholic *Sauer* or *Alte Most* could be bottled and stored, and available throughout the year. But the freshly pressed, non-alcoholic version was only available directly from the press. Groups who wanted to revel in this seasonal treat undertook a *Bummel* (a leisurely trip) to restaurants in apple-rich regions to enjoy the drink.

GLÜHMOST (Serves 10)

This mulled cider is a wonderful alternative to the heady and alcoholic *Glühweins* of the Christmas season (though you can always use boozy cider if you like).

2 liters/8 cups apple juice or cider
    (alcoholic or not)
2 each of oranges and lemons
A pinkie-sized nub of ginger, peeled and
    cut in half
4 cloves
2 each of cinnamon sticks and star anise
1 vanilla bean, sliced open

Fill a large pot with the apple juice or cider. With a vegetable peeler, peel off a few thin sections of orange and lemon rind (try to avoid the bitter white pith) and juice the fruit. Add this, plus the rest of the ingredients, to the pot, then warm over medium heat, being careful to not let boil.

Träsch

Träsch in most Swiss German dialects, or *Bätzi* in Bernese German, is a spirit distilled from apples and pears. Both names refer to fruit leftovers—*Bätzi*—which can mean apple core, and *Träsch*, from *Trester*, which means the leftover parts of the fruits once they'd been pressed for juice or oil. Similarly, apple and pear spirits would be distilled from the pressing leftovers to make *Most* (cider). Today, the whole fruit is typically used.

Whereas *Träsch* is the rustic, catch-all term for apple or pear *Schnaps*, when a certain kind of apple or pear is used, the spirit is referred to by its variety—like the Williams pear or Gravenstein apple. Not all kinds of *Träsch* are created equally. Farmers may simply leave a big vat of apples and pears to ferment in a barn, however fine spirit producers carefully choose their fruit.

WILLIAM TELL

40 ml/1.3 fl oz Träsch
20 ml/0.7 fl oz cinnamon syrup
20 ml/0.7 fl oz lemon juice
120 ml/4 fl oz Saurer Most (dry apple cider)
Cinnamon

Shake the *Träsch*, syrup and lemon juice with ice. Strain and top with *Saurer Most*. Sprinkle with cinnamon.

APPLE SHOT

Fill a shot glass with half *Träsch*, half *Süssmost*. Sprinkle with cinnamon.

Top, the team at Mosterei Kobelt: (L-R) Petra, Geoffrey, Jennifer, Karen, and Ruedi Kobelt

Mosterei Kobelt

When you arrive in Marbach, canton St. Gallen, it's hard to miss the three giant cider bottles sitting along the main road. They point the way to Mosterei Kobelt, the *"kleinste Mosterei der Schweiz"* (the smallest cidery in Switzerland). Deep in the heart of the Rhine Valley, a region famous for its apples, Kobelt has been pressing fruit into cider since 1906 and has a cult following among locals and discerning cider-lovers throughout the country.

When I poke my head into their well-stocked shop, the smiling face of Jennifer Kobelt greets me. Jennifer, along with her brother Geoffrey, are the fifth generation of cider-makers, and they will soon take over from their parents, Ruedi and Karen, who have managed the Mosterei since 1985.

"We're in the last two weeks of production," says Jennifer, as she leads me through the production facility and the stages of cider making, "and we'll be finished with the apples in early November." She shows me the chute where the apples are sorted, the giant press from the 1970s that can only be cleaned by getting a large flashlight and climbing inside, and the chilly rooms where the juice is stored throughout the year.

"Nothing here is concentrate, it's all pure juice."

Back in their cozy shop, we peek into their tasting room, decorated with old bottles of Kobelt cider and factory supplies. It's a mini *Most* museum. "It's all the old stuff we found in the Mosterei and didn't know what to do with," she says, laughing. But it looks wonderful and points to the history of the place.

Like in many parts of Switzerland, the processing of apples into juice, cider and *Schnaps* was an important part of farm life, and the Mosterei was a community hub. The farmers would bring their apples to be pressed into cider and their fermented fruit distilled, but they would also meet and chat. The whole region was, historically, agricultural, with much of the land dominated by farms.

"The hills were covered in trees," says Ruedi Kobelt, called over by his daughter Jennifer to weigh in. Now there are fewer, and the consumption of *Most*, along with alcoholic beverages in general, is down. "Some of the old guys would come in and buy a two liter bottle of *Schnaps* every week. But it's rarer now." Plus the consumers are getting savvier.

"People want to know what they are consuming. They appreciate that the apples are regional, and that we don't use concentrate."

Geoffrey comes in wearing orange gloves, and signals to Ruedi. Outside a giant neon green truck full of apples has pulled up.

"That one is on the larger side," says Jennifer, motioning to the truck. Suddenly there is a scrum of people sorting through the apples being funneled out of the truck onto the chute. Different generations together, harmonious... the way it's been for over a century.

Swiss Spirits

Alchemy—its goals were straightforward: find a universal solvent, find the elixir of life, turn lead into gold.

Alchemists were determined to extract the "spirit" of a liquid in a bid to find its essence, and possibly the elixir of life. After learning about distillation from Arab scholars, Europeans began the process of separating the alcohol from fermented beverages—first turning wine into brandy.

The name for this distillate came from the Latin for water of life, *aqua vitae*, like the Italian *acquavite* or French *eau-de-vie*. In German, it can be called *Geist* (spirit) or *Branntwein* (literally burned wine), referring to the distillation process.

In the Middle Ages, spirits were the domain of doctors and apothecaries, and used primarily for medicinal purposes. As time passed, spirits made their way into restaurants, bars, and the home.

But spirits were not always welcome in wider society. Seeing the negative effects of overindulgence led the Swiss government to heavily regulate alcohol throughout the 20th century.

Regulating Spirits

These spirited additions to daily life were not universally accepted. In 1887 the Swiss Alcohol Board (SAB), a government department responsible for the production and distribution of hard alcohol and industrial ethanol (though not beer or wine), was formed.

The backlash against *Schnaps* had already begun decades before. In 1837, Heinrich Zschokke published the *Branntweinpest* (The *Schnaps* Plague) and two years later Jeremias Gotthelf wrote *Wie fünf Mädchen im Branntwein jämmerlich umkommen* (How Five Girls Perished Miserably in *Schnaps*). Alcohol abuse was seen as a problem of the working classes—farmers, factory workers, and the poor.

Initially, the government's target was to control potato *Schnaps* (*Härdöpfler*). Also known as *Kartoffelbrand*, potato *Schnaps* has been distilled in Switzerland since the 1800s. Easy to grow and cheaper than wine, potatoes were the most popular choice for distilling, at a time when hard liquor was consumed at a much higher rate than today. For many who lived in poverty, *Härdöpfler* provided not only a way to still hunger pangs, but also to escape a bleak existence.

But the government was concerned.

Potatoes were a nutritious complex carbohydrate, and the government saw their metamorphosis into booze as a threat to the food supply. Shortly after the First World War, the government banned the use of potatoes as a *Schnaps* base. However, much like absinthe, many people continued to distill their tubers in secret. It wasn't until almost the 21st century that it could legally be produced again.

The SAB worked hard to promote the consumption of crops as food rather than alcoholic drinks. They incentivized making *Süssmost*—sweet, non-alcoholic apple juice—instead of distilling apples, and they ran ads promoting healthy eating in an attempt to encourage the Swiss public to eat their fruit and potatoes rather than distill them.

"Eat an apple during your morning break!" declared one ad, with a row of smiling children biting into crisp fruit. Fruit and vegetables were the key to happiness and good health, and one campaign even proclaimed *Kartoffeln machen schlank* (potatoes make you slim), encouraging women to eat, rather than drink, their taters.

Mobile Distilleries

Swiss farmers were allowed to distill a certain amount of spirits, based on the number of cattle they had on the farm. The booze was meant to be used for farm purposes—when calves had colic, as a disinfectant, or even historically to pay farm hands.

However, Swiss farmers didn't all have stills in their barns to turn their fruit into *Schnaps*. Instead, they depended on mobile distilleries—often big carts with stills on the back, pulled by horses or tractors.

After the fall harvest, the farmers would put their fruit in big barrels where it could ferment. Between the New Year and the spring, travelling distilleries would go from farm to farm distilling this fermented mash into alcohol. For smaller operations it would take a day or so, but my father-in-law remembers the cart staying at his parent's farm for a whole week before all their fruit had been processed.

Some of these traveling distillers would be above board, checking government cards as they went, and only distilling as much as each farm was allowed. But there were also black-market distillers, who would be willing to go over the allowed limit or secretly distill extra fruit.

Today these mobile distilleries still exist in some form, though they distill much less than they used to. And they don't travel to each farm anymore; typically, they set up shop in one location and local farmers come to them, with their fermented mash in tow.

Kirsch

Kirsch is Switzerland's most famous spirit. It has a long history, both as a favored tipple gracing soldiers' flasks and hiking rucksacks, and an enemy of the temperance movement, who saw the damage it could do to heavy imbibers.

Cherry trees were brought to Switzerland from the Middle East by crusaders, and today they blossom throughout the country. Kirsch is made in most regions; most famously in cantons Basel and Zug.

In central Switzerland alone, there are more than 300 varieties of cherry, and over 800 in the whole country. For one liter/34 fl oz of kirsch, upwards of 3000 cherries are needed. The cherries are fermented with their stones and, in some cases, this gives the kirsch a light almond taste.

Owing to its relatively neutral flavor, kirsch is often used in cooking and baking. It's added to cheese fondue and some people even have little shot glasses of kirsch next to their plates, to dunk the bread before dipping it into the cheese. It also features in confections like *Kirschstängeli* (booze filled chocolate sticks) as well as numerous cakes like Black Forest cake and *Zuger Kirschtorte*. For a taste of the cake in drink form, try this:

ZUGER KIRSCHTORTE

40 ml/1.3 fl oz Röteli or other
  cherry liqueur
40 ml/1.3 fl oz amaretto
40 ml/1.3 fl oz cream
20 ml/0.7 fl oz kirsch

Shake with ice, then strain into a glass.

ROSE

This is a classic cocktail that is made with kirsch. If you don't have strawberry syrup, substitute with another red syrup like grenadine, cherry, or raspberry.

60 ml/2 fl oz dry vermouth
30 ml/1.3 fl oz kirsch
15 ml/0.5 fl oz strawberry syrup

Shake with ice, then strain into a glass.

Kirschtopf

Another fruity, boozy favorite is the *Kirschtopf* (like a *Rumtopf*, only with kirsch). Large grey and blue ceramic pots are filled with seasonal fruit throughout the growing season, and topped with good-quality kirsch. Then throughout the winter the boozy fruit can be poured over ice cream and spooned onto crepes, the liquid being drunk to the last.

If you want to make your own *Kirschtopf*, get a large container (glass or ceramic work best). As soon as seasonal strawberries are ready, place 500 g/1 lb washed and de-stemmed berries in a bowl with 250 g/½ lb sugar and wait an hour. Then add it to your pot along with 750 ml/3 cups kirsch. When the next fruit is ripe (cherries or apricots), do the same, adding 250 g/½ lb sugar for every 500g/1 lb fruit, and topping it off with 250 ml/1 cup kirsch, always making sure that the fruits are completely covered by the kirsch. You can keep doing this until you have filled your pot, adding raspberries, plums, peaches and pears along the way. Once the last fruit has been added, wait a week, add an additional 250 ml/1 cup of kirsch, then cover and let sit for at least a month.

Use fruit that is ripe, but never moldy. Always keep your pot in a cool cellar and make sure the alcohol is covering the fruit. Some fruits to avoid are bananas, citrus and melons.

Abricotine

Switzerland's favorite apricots come from Valais, the warm wine-producing region in the southwest of the country. They are the pride of Swiss fruit production, with stands selling the scarlet speckled fruits popping up throughout the country in July and August.

The most famous variety is the *Luizet*, named for the French horticulturist who developed them. They thrive in the warm, dry conditions of Valais, but their short season and delicate fruit mean that they are usually not transported very far from where they are picked.

It's this variety that is used to make *Abricotine*, the strong apricot spirit of the region. It's a protected product and for a producer to be able to use the name *Abricotine*, 90% of the fruits must be *Luizet* apricots, and all aspects of production must take place in the Valais.

ABRICOTINE SPRITZER

40 ml/1.3 fl oz Abricotine
A thread of saffron
15 ml/0.5 fl oz lemon juice
1 tbsp apricot jam, strained
Chilled sparkling white wine

Steep the saffron in the *Abricotine* for about 10 minutes. Remove the saffron and place the liquid, lemon juice and jam in an ice-filled cocktail shaker. Shake well and strain. Pour into a glass and top with sparkling wine.

Munder saffron

High on a Valais mountain is the tiny community of Mund, where they harvest no more than 5 kg/11 lb of saffron per year. Saffron grows from crocus flowers, each bloom yielding only three thin scarlet threads. It takes over 100 flowers to make a single gram, which can cost upwards of 30 francs.

It's thought that during the Middle Ages the saffron was brought to Switzerland from Spain by pilgrims, who smuggled it into the country in their hair and beards.

Today it is as revered as ever, and you can purchase strands of saffron from Mund, as well as saffron *Schnaps* and liqueur.

Pflümli and Zwetschgen

Pflümli and Zwetschgen both refer to spirits made from plums: Pflümli typically designating round plums, and Zwetschgen the harder, oval variety (prune plums). After cherries, plums are the most popular stone fruit for distilling in Switzerland. Many varieties exist—including spirits made from little golden mirabelles, and the Chézard and Bérudge plums from Neuchâtel. There is also the Vieille Prune, a version that is sweetened and aged in barrels to produce a fragrant, golden spirit.

An integral part of many beloved Swiss winter drinks—like Holdrio (rosehip tea and Zwetschgen) and Schümli Pflümli (coffee, Pflümli and whipped cream)—plum brandy is kept on hand by most restaurants.

Damassine

One of Switzerland's finest plum brandies comes from the Jura where they grow little red plums called damasson rouge. As the name hints, they were brought back by the crusaders—damasson, like the city of Damascus.

Grown throughout the region, particularly in the Ajoie, these little ruby plums produce a superb eau-de-vie. In the early 2000s, Damassine was granted protected status with strict guidelines about how the spirit is to be made, including a stipulation that the plums must be collected once they have fallen off the tree naturally. No shaking or picking allowed!

Zwetschgen can be replaced with any kind of plum brandy in the following drinks.

PLUM STINGER

30 ml/1 fl oz Zwetschgen
30 ml/1 fl oz Crème de Menthe

Shake with ice.

PLUM AND CHERRY

30 ml/1 fl oz Zwetschgen
30 ml/1 fl oz Röteli or another cherry liqueur
15 ml/0.5 fl oz vanilla or cinnamon simple
   syrup
1 egg white (optional)
Sparkling white or rosé wine

Shake everything except the wine in the cocktail shaker, first dry (if you are using egg whites) then with ice. Strain and top with sparkling wine.

PLUM SIDECAR

40 ml/1.3 fl oz Zwetschgen
30 ml/1 fl oz Grand Marnier
20 ml/0.7 fl oz lemon juice
20 ml/0.7 fl oz orange juice

Shake with ice. Strain and garnish with lemon or orange peel.

Williams Tonic

Williams

Basically any food or drink in Switzerland with Williams in the name means that it contains pear or pear *Schnaps*.

This is down to the name of the pear itself, the Williams pear (Bartlett in North America) which, with its firm-ish texture and juicy flesh, lends itself well to cooking and processing. The pears carry the surname of Williams, the English gardener who popularized them in the UK. Later, an American named Enoch Bartlett acquired a piece of property in Massachusetts full of Williams pear trees that had been brought over from England. He didn't know their provenance, so he simply named the variety after himself. It wasn't until decades later in the early 1800s that people realized that the two pears were the same variety.

Pears in bottles

Williams pears are the basis for the *Schnaps* of the same name, and it was the Germanier family in canton Valais who first had the idea of enhancing their pear spirit by growing an entire pear inside the liquor bottle. The Germaniers carefully placed their bottles over tiny pear blossoms on the tree and let the pear grow inside, gently removing the bottles from the tree once the fruit was ripe. Although today there are knockoffs with false bottoms allowing fully grown pears to be added, some distilleries in Switzerland, France, and Germany still practice the original method.

Once you've finished your bottle, don't be tempted to break it open and fish out the pear—by that time it doesn't have any flavor and smashing the bottle makes quite a mess.

AMARETTO PERA

50 ml/1.7 fl oz Williams
30 ml/1 fl oz amaretto
20 ml/0.7 fl oz lemon juice

Shake with ice.

WILLIAMS TONIC

Williams makes a great replacement to gin—this is a favorite from Distillery Studer, a traditional Swiss fruit brandy producer in canton Lucerne (see next page).

30 ml/1 fl oz Williams
Tonic water
1 Lemon peel

Pour the Williams over ice and top with tonic water. Rub the rim of the glass with lemon peel and drop in.

Distillery Studer

We have a pretty full liquor cabinet. This is partly thanks to one person—my sister-in-law, Franziska, who works at Studer, a family-run, award-winning distillery in canton Lucerne.

Studer was founded in 1883 and, having initially produced confectionery rather than spirits, transitioned to *Schnaps* in the early 20th century after a fire at the factory. They were pioneers in barrel-ageing their high-quality fruit spirits. In 1970, they were the first Swiss distillers to produce *Vieille Prune* by ageing their best plum brandy. In 1981, they made a pear version, *Vielle Poire Williams*; most likely the first barrel-aged pear brandy in the world.

Making fruit spirits takes much more time and effort than making other kinds of spirits. Distilling from grains, potatoes and other starches is relatively straightforward, but distilling fruit requires much more attention to the quality of the raw product. A distillery like Studer, which aims for the highest quality fruit *Schnaps* possible, has to have perfectly ripe, flavorful fruit.

First, the fruit is harvested (a lot of Studer's comes from orchards in Valais) then stored at the distillery until it reaches peak ripeness. Every day, the distillery manager takes several fruit from different parts of the pallets. When he deems them perfectly ripe the production begins.

The fruit is washed and set along a conveyor belt so any leaves, twigs, or rot can be removed by hand. The harvest needs to be processed as soon as possible, so the employees of the distillery work overtime and weekends until all the fruit is safely tucked away in fermenting vats. Six to eight weeks later, the mash is ready to be distilled. Afterwards, some can already be bottled, and the rest gets filled into wooden barrels to develop additional flavor or is further processed into fruit liqueurs.

Sadly, the market for a lot of traditional Swiss *Schnaps* is decreasing. Spirits like *Zwetschgen*, *Träsch*, and Williams are losing ground to rum, gin, and flavored vodka. Smart distilleries like Studer have widened their product range, making interesting new products, like vermouth, or low-alcohol options alongside the more traditional Swiss spirits. It's a shame though, because Switzerland's glorious fruit spirits are delicious and they mix well into many cocktails.

BIRNEL

Berlin-based bartender and cocktail festival founder Robert Schröter spent some time at Studer and very kindly made this very Swiss drink for the book. *Birnel* is a syrup made from pears, traditional in central Switzerland.

50 ml/1.7 fl oz high quality pear eau-de-vie
   (his favorite is Studer Williams Supérieur)
10 ml/0.3 fl oz Birnel
1 dash Angostura bitters
Pear slices as garnish

Stir with ice in a glass.

Top right, Jonathan Schönberger; middle right, Reto Meier; bottom right, Ivano Friedli-Studer

Chapter 7: From the Farms

Home Remedies and Love Potions

Mothers and grandmothers are the keepers of secrets, in charge of the most important knowledge on the farm, like how to prepare a home remedy and how to prepare a love potion.

Maybe you'll find a recipe in a worn and much-loved book with yellowing pages, or taped to the back of a cupboard door. Perhaps nothing was ever written down at all, and it's just a memory of how hands stirred or seasoned, how long you had to wait, or how many bubbles would appear.

Regardless, it's all there; from grandmother to mother to daughter: the best herbal mix for upset stomachs, how long to store the syrupy liqueur and what bottles to store it in, the exact mix that had encouraged grandfather to linger in the evening...

Remedial Drinks

Chrüter

Kräuterschnaps (herb *Schnaps*) is a twice-distilled spirit flavored with a mix of herbs and spices. The process is simple: distill a spirit—apple, pear, or quince will do—then mix in cumin, anise and a secret formulation of other herbs and spices. Distill again and voilà—*Chrüter*. It isn't just for the liquor cabinet; it can also be found in the medicine cabinet and applied liberally to bad moods, stomachaches, and general digestive problems.

Alte Chrüter

There is also *Alte* (aged) *Chrüter*. Roasted wood chips and a bit of sugar are added to regular *Chrüter*, creating a sweeter, more flavorful, and slightly milder drink.

Bürgermeisterli

The Basel version of *Chrüter* is named after a former *Bürgermeister* (mayor) of the city, who made his own herby spirit at the end of the 18th century.

VERDAUERLI

A *Verdauerli* is simply the Swiss German word for digestif—a small tipple to take after a big meal to help with the *Verdauung* (digestion). A variation on the theme is this warm drink that contains the digestive magic of tea, honey and herby booze.

30 ml/2 tbsp Chrüter
1 tsp honey
Peppermint or fennel tea

Place the *Chrüter* and honey in a mug, then fill to the top with hot tea.

Chümmi/Äntäbüsi

Flavored with *Kümmel* (caraway), this *Schnaps* is popular throughout central Switzerland. My in-laws drink a version called *Äntäbüsi*, a dialect name which literally means duck (*Ente*) and cat (*Büsi*). The origin story is about feuding farmers, a caraway windfall, and a cat that lived in harmony with ducklings. Inspired by the cordial relations between cat and ducklings, the farmers decided to let bygones be bygones over a glass of *Schnaps* but, unable to choose between *Chümmi* and *Chrüter*, they mixed them together and forgot their differences.

CHÜMMI

500 ml/2 cups kirsch
2 tbsp sugar
1 tbsp caraway seeds, crushed

Place everything in a large jar, shake well and leave in a warm place for up to a month, shaking occasionally. Strain into a bottle.

Chörbliwasser

The slightly sparkling *Chörbliwasser* is a twice-distilled drink that tastes of licorice and is used medicinally—distilled, but non-alcoholic. The flavor comes from the addition of *myrrhis odorata* (sweet cicely), and it was traditionally prepared in two disparate regions of Switzerland—the Rhine valley in St. Gallen, and the Emmental in Bern.

Chörbliwasser has been applied to rashes and other skin conditions, as well as open wounds, as a mild disinfectant. Dentists would suggest their patients gargle it to relieve infections in the mouth and enthusiasts claim it purifies their blood, lowers blood pressure and relieves joint pain.

You can still find *Chörbliwasser* today—the best-known producer is the family-run Distillery Zogg in canton St. Gallen, which has a purpose-built *Chörbliwasser* still and has been supplying the region for decades. I visited the distillery at the end of summer, when a new batch had just been distilled, and bought a bottle of the milky-white liquid, feeling lucky because they sell out quickly.

"Drink it with tea," Mathias Zogg, one of the co-owners, told me, "and more than a shot a day is probably too much."

Eierkirsch

Eierkirsch is a kirsch-based drink with added eggs, cream and sugar. At Christmas, it can be spiced with cinnamon and nutmeg.

But it's not just a holiday drink. Produced year-round on the same farms that would grow the cherries needed for kirsch, the addition of eggs and sugar was not only to create a pleasing taste, but also to provide protein and energy for the laborers who worked on the farm.

My mother-in-law, Josy, fondly remembers drinking cold, refreshing *Eierkirsch* during the *Heuen* when her family would cut and dry the hay for the cows.

EIERKIRSCH

4 egg yolks
90 g/3 oz condensed milk
150 ml/⅔ cup milk
1 tbsp vanilla paste (or the seeds of
    one vanilla pod)
150 ml/⅔ cup kirsch

Whisk together the yolks, condensed milk, milk and vanilla in a large bowl.

Place the bowl over a pot of simmering water on medium-low heat (the bottom of the bowl should not touch the water), and cook, whisking, until it has thickened and is hot to the touch with a temperature of 70°C/160°F. Be patient; depending on the heat this can take a while (just don't let it get too hot or the eggs will scramble).

Take it off the heat and whisk in the kirsch.

Let cool briefly, then funnel into a bottle and store in the fridge. It keeps for about a week.

SNOWBALL

One famous mixed drink that uses *Eierkirsch* is the boozy, eggnoggy Snowball.

100 ml/3.4 fl oz Elmer Citro or
    other fizzy lemonade
20 ml/0.7 fl oz lime juice or
    lime cordial
60 ml/2 fl oz Eierkirsch
Maraschino cherries as garnish

Fill a tall glass with ice. Pour in the lemonade and lime juice, then top with *Eierkirsch*. Stir lightly and garnish with maraschino cherries.

Rosoli

Rosoli is a cherry liqueur found in central Switzerland, especially in the village of Einsiedeln. According to historian Kurt Lussi, this drink originated in Padua, Italy, in the 14th century. In the 18th century, out of necessity, central Swiss farmers took their cows to market in northern Italy and brought back this sweetened *Schnaps*. It became linked with the Swiss tradition of *kilten* (courting your lady love). Late in the evening, bachelors would knock on the windows of their sweethearts, who would, in turn, offer them nips of their homemade *Rosoli*. Eventually this sweet love potion would be used as a dash of courage to help elicit a marriage proposal.

Although today most production of *Rosoli* is done by farming families using secret recipes passed down through the generations, you can still buy *Einsiedler Ur-Rosoli*. You can also make your own using fresh or dried cherries. The recipe I like best is mentioned by Kurt Lussi in his book on love potions, *Liebestrünke*, and comes from the *Nidwaldner Brattig* (a regional yearbook) from 1936.

ROSOLI

150 g/5 oz dried cherries
500 ml/2 cups water
200 g/1 cup sugar
1 cinnamon stick
250 ml/1 cup kirsch or other
*   clear fruit brandy*

Put the cherries in a large jar. Bring the water, sugar and cinnamon stick to a boil. Make sure all the sugar is dissolved, then take off the heat. Pour the liquid over the dried cherries, mix well, and let sit for two days. Strain and add the kirsch, mixing well, then funnel into bottles and store in a cool, dry place. Makes about 500 ml/2 cups.

The sweet, syrupy leftover cherries make a great ice cream topping, or use them to garnish the cocktails.

Röteli

Röteli is a similar liqueur made with dried cherries and spices that dates from at least the 19th century. It was traditionally made by families in Graubünden, each using a different spice mixture. In the early 1900s, traditional recipes were collected and experimented with, leading to a standardized version that could be mass produced.

It's traditional to drink *Röteli* on New Year's Eve. In the olden days, bachelors would take this occasion to go from farmhouse to farmhouse visiting farmers' unmarried daughters. At each farm they would sample a glass of *Röteli* that the single ladies (under the watchful eye of their mothers) had made.

Some saw the drink as a kind of love potion, and often these visits would eventually result in marriage proposals. The further into the valley the bachelors went, the drunker they got, and the better looking and more appealing the daughters became, giving a big advantage to those who lived in remote farmhouses.

Röteli: a cautionary tale
For me, *Röteli* is synonymous with one of the most harrowing nights of my life.

It was New Year's Eve, and my Swiss family suggested tobogganing in Graubünden. As a Canadian, my experience with tobogganing was extensive—just beyond my backyard as a child was a large and popular hill where we would go nearly every snowy day. I was eager to try tobogganing in Switzerland, and my cousin's girlfriend excitedly told me how you could sled down for almost a half hour. Wow! That must be some hill.

At around 6:00 p.m., we took a bus up a steep and winding road to a little chalet restaurant full of families celebrating the New Year. It was a grand time. At the end of the meal the server brought around a bottle and started pouring shots.

"Have you ever had *Röteli* before?"

I hadn't… and it was delicious. I let him pour me a second. Then a third. My cousin's girlfriend turned to me, saying, "You'd better slow down, you'll have to navigate!"

I giggled. It doesn't take too much to navigate a big hill. After the drinks, and toasting the New Year, we gathered outside the chalet. Then everything changed.

People started getting out headlamps.

"What are the headlamps for?" I asked my cousin.

"To help you navigate," he said, handing me one.

"Are there no floodlights on the hill?" I asked.

He gave me a funny look. "There aren't any lights on the road."

"The road?"

Everyone was walking over to the place where the buses had come up the mountain. The families that had been in the chalet were starting to steer their sleds down along the winding, slippery road. My cousin handed me a toboggan. I gingerly got on the sled, adjusted my head lamp, dug my heels into the snow, and went about five meters/16 feet when a family with a grandmother and two school-aged children blew past me, whooping and hollering. This was going to be a long half hour.

As I quickly learned, navigation was indeed key. At the end of each straightaway you had to negotiate a sharp turn, otherwise you would be flung off into the forest.

Then came the buses.

Buses were carrying people back up the road, and when you saw their headlights, you had to throw yourself into the side of the mountain to avoid being crushed under their wheels.

At the bottom of the hill I was white-knuckled and teary. My cousin smiled at me. "Oh well," he said, "your year can only go up from here."

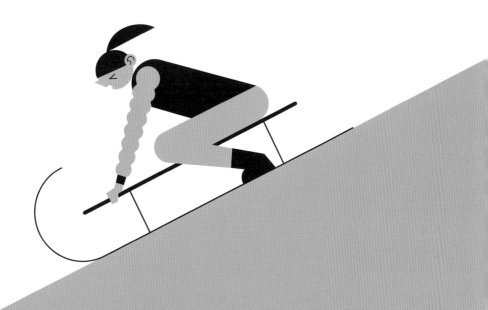

Cheers to Cherries!

Although traditionally it was typically drunk alone, *Röteli* and *Rosoli* are essentially cherry liqueurs and mix well into soda, as well as classic cocktails.

CHERRY COLA FLOAT

The classic North American float with soda gets a Swiss twist.

Add two scoops of vanilla ice cream and one shot *Röteli* or *Rosoli* to a tall glass. Top with cola.

BÜNDNER RIVELLA

Stir a shot (or two) of *Röteli* into a glass of Rivella.

CHERRY OLD FASHIONED

1 tsp cherry syrup
30 ml/1 fl oz Röteli or Rosoli
2 dashes bitters (preferably orange)
50 ml/1.7 fl oz bourbon

Mix together the cherry syrup, *Röteli/Rosoli* and bitters in a glass. Add ice, pour in the bourbon and stir until it's well chilled. If desired, add a splash of sparkling water. Garnish with orange and cherries.

CHERRY MANHATTAN

50 ml/1.7 fl oz whiskey
20 ml/0.7 fl oz sweet vermouth
20 ml/0.7 fl oz Röteli or Rosoli
3 dashes bitters

Shake all ingredients together with ice. Garnish with cherries.

Cherry Old Fashioned

Turning flax into linen, the old-fashioned way, at the modern Brächete in Zäziwil

Brächete

Before the ease of readily available cotton, Swiss farming families would make linen by hand by processing flax. The breaking, or *Brächete* as it was called, was a day-long event.

Using large wooden implements, the flax would be combed, roasted, rolled through a large wooden crushing machine, pounded by hand, combed again, rinsed, and spun into threads as fine as hair. Finally it could be woven into all manner of products, from tablecloths to *Trachten* (traditional Swiss dresses). No part of the flax went to waste and byproducts were used for house and pipe insulation, as well as in sausage making.

All this hard work demanded a proper reward at the end of the day, and that came via a strong caramel *Schnaps—Brächere Brönnts*, named for the event it was served at. As dusk fell, the exhausted flax breakers would imbibe the rejuvenating liquid, play their accordions, and dance into the night. Love also blossomed, as the villagers waited to see which young man carried home which young lady's spinning wheel.

You can still attend a modern version of the *Brächete*, which is held on the last Wednesday in September in the Emmental town of Zäziwil. Locals in traditional dress demonstrate all the stages of linen production by hand, and there's a lively market too. It is probably the only place you might find *Brächere Brönnts* outside of private homes.

Hanna Stalder, a member of the organizing committee of the modern *Brächete*, has been making *Brächere Brönnts* for decades. According to her there's no standard recipe: each family makes their own version. And they drink it differently too, and not only during the *Brächete*.

"I like to have a sip when I feel a cold coming on," she says. "Sorts me right out."

BRÄCHERE BRÖNNTS

150 g/¾ cup sugar
200 ml/¾ cup water
3 cloves
3 juniper berries
1 tsp caraway seeds
1 cinnamon stick
400 ml/1⅔ cups kirsch

Measure your sugar into a large pot—you want an even layer. Have your water measured out and ready, next to the stove.

Over high heat, begin to caramelize the sugar. When the bottom layer liquefies, or starts to smoke at the sides, use a wooden spoon to stir it all together. If you have the feeling that it is too hot, or that the color is changing too quickly, pull it off the heat and keep stirring.

Keep stirring as all the sugar liquefies and turns golden.

As soon as it starts to turn amber, add the water. This will stop the caramel from cooking and darkening further, but it will splutter and the caramel will seize up.

Put the pot back over medium high heat and cook until all the sugar dissolves in the water. Keep stirring it gently; this might take a few minutes.

Take off the heat, add the cloves, juniper berries, caraway seeds, and cinnamon stick, and let sit for about 15 minutes.

Fill a large measuring cup with the kirsch. Strain the caramel into the cup and stir.

Funnel into a clean bottle. Makes about 500 ml/2 cups. Serve your Brächere Brönnts straight or mix it into cinnamon tea.

TIPS

• Making caramel can be intimidating—never leave it unattended on the stove, as it often cooks faster than you think.
• I like to use kirsch but other spirits with low flavor (vodka) or something like Williams or Zwetschgen would also work.
• With all the sugar and booze, this should keep indefinitely in your liquor cabinet.

Val-de-Travers

Chapter 8:
From Illegal Stills

Absinthe

Absinthe originated in the Val-de-Travers, in the canton of Neuchâtel. It's made from a blend of anise, fennel, wormwood, and other botanicals.

During the late 1800s, absinthe became the drink of choice for the bohemians in Paris, and the likes of Baudelaire, Toulouse-Lautrec, Zola, and Gauguin imbibed the spirit, known as "The Green Fairy."

Although many of its psychoactive properties were exaggerated (or can be attributed to the fact that many artists mixed their absinthe with laudanum and other drugs), the tide turned on absinthe at the start of the 20th century and tales of mania led to it being banned for almost a century.

In Switzerland, it was one farmer whose murderous rampage spurred the ban. Jean Lanfray came home drunk one afternoon and when his wife refused to polish his shoes, he shot her and their two young daughters with a shotgun. Two small glasses of absinthe were blamed, though Lanfray was a known inebriate who had already drunk over a liter of wine and numerous spirits before he arrived home.

Outrage about the case led to a popular vote in Switzerland on whether the government should ban the drink. Unions, churches and doctors rallied against the drink, accusing it of leading to a general degradation of morals and values. In 1908, the vote passed with 63.5%, and many European and North American countries followed suit.

Starting in the late 1990s, absinthe has had a revival in Europe and North America. In 2005, the Swiss repealed the earlier ban and absinthe was again made (legally) in its birthplace, the Val-de-Travers.

Rebel Fairy

Although absinthe was banned for nearly a century, production never stopped in Val-de-Travers. Stills remained in basements, and herbs—anise, fennel, wormwood—were dried in attics. If a formal complaint was lodged, the police would come to the house, destroy the still, pour out the absinthe and issue a fine. To distill and drink absinthe was seen as an act of resistance.

How to serve absinthe

Place the absinthe in a glass. Rest an absinthe spoon (or regular fork) on top of the glass and place a sugar cube on it. Slowly pour cold water through the sugar cube—the drink will get cloudy. Stir and enjoy.

This method is known as *la louche* (French for opaque) because the clear liquid gets cloudy as the water is added.

What doesn't kill you...

Over the centuries, people have praised and denounced absinthe for the effect it has on the human body. It has been seen as a cause of mental illness and numerous other disorders, yet before it was condemned as an instrument for murder, absinthe, and more generally wormwood, were said to have curative properties.

Here are some of the things it purported to do: cure toothaches, seasickness, shrew and scorpion bites, stomach troubles, scurvy, cholera and the plague, prevent menstrual cramps and mental illness, be the antidote for poisonous mushrooms, remove worms in the ears, and prevent beer from spoiling.

BOTTOMS UP!

The history of this clandestine distilling, as well as the history of absinthe itself before and after the ban, is catalogued in the excellent museum, Maison de l'Absinthe, in Môtiers in the heart of the Val-de-Travers. They also showcase all the absinthes produced in the region, and you can taste them too.

Maison de l'Absinthe, canton Neuchâtel

Absinthe and Mitterrand

In 1983, it was a big deal when Pierre Aubert, the Swiss president, invited French president François Mitterrand to have lunch in Neuchâtel: it was France's first state visit to Switzerland since 1910. The meal, hosted at the Hôtel DuPeyrou, was meticulously planned—melon and ham, local trout, and *Soufflé glacé à la Fée Verte* (Green Fairy ice cream soufflé) for dessert. When the chef was interviewed about it on television, he gave up its "secret" ingredient—absinthe.

Still banned in Switzerland, the chef was eventually taken to court, where he said that the dessert hadn't contained absinthe at all, but the anise-flavored Pastis. However, instead of being charged for possession of absinthe, he was charged with fraud. He was eventually acquitted, two years later.

Here's a taste of Mitterrand's dessert, without having to make a soufflé.

FRAPPÉ À LA FÉE VERTE

50 ml/1.7 fl oz Eierkirsch
50 ml/1.7 fl oz absinthe
200 ml/6.7 fl oz milk
2 scoops vanilla ice cream (about
  100 g/¼ cup)

Blend well.

It was in New Orleans that absinthe was mixed into some of the finest cocktails. Here are two classics: boozy, bold Sazerac, and milky green *Suissesse*, which is creamy and refreshing and makes an excellent brunch drink (or hair of the dog).

SWISS SAZERAC

40 ml/1.3 fl oz cognac
20 ml/0.7 fl oz whiskey or bourbon
20 ml/0.7 fl oz absinthe
20 ml/0.7 fl oz simple syrup
10 ml/0.3 fl oz Alpenbitter

Pour everything into a glass filled with ice and stir.

SUISSESSE

45 ml/1.5 fl oz absinthe
30 ml/1 fl oz Crème de Menthe
30 ml/1 fl oz cream
1 egg white

Shake with ice and strain into a glass.

Frappé à la Fée Verte

Chapter 9: From the Alpine Meadows

The Swiss love their herbal remedies, and they brew and distil many drinks that rely on the flavors and effects of plants, notably those found in the Alps. Some are only found at high altitudes, like edelweiss; some are Alpine relatives of more common plants, like Alpine wormwood; and others, like peppermint and chamomile, grow happily down in the valleys as well. Plenty of the plants have centuries-old purported medicinal applications and are used to treat everything from inflammation and indigestion to bad breath and bad dreams.

Here are some plants commonly found in Alpine herb mixes:

chamomile

rose hip

sage

thyme

gentian root

verbena

lemon balm

peppermint

lady's mantel

nettle

dandelion

wall germander

plantain

hyssop

mallow

yarrow

edelweiss

juniper

Alpine Spirits

Gentian liqueur

Originating just over the border in the French Alps, this aromatic liqueur is made from the roots of the yellow gentian plant (not to be confused with the stemless gentian—the bright blue, trumpet-shaped flower that, alongside fuzzy edelweiss, is the symbol of Alpine flora). Known as *Enzian* in German, it's been a popular drink in the Alpine region for centuries, especially from the mid-17th to early 19th centuries. Today you can buy regional varieties of this bitter, aromatic drink and many people enjoy a shot after a big meal.

Genepi

This is a sweetened liqueur made from Alpine wormwood, sometimes known as white genepi. Light yellow-green in color, it is aromatic and drunk as both an aperitif or digestif.

Edelweiss

You can also find *Schnaps* made from the country's beloved, furry edelweiss. With a very light taste of honey, and not too bitter, it's a fragrant taste of the Alps.

Heuschnaps

Some *Schnaps* also add hay (*Heu*) as a flavoring. *Heuschnaps* from the Wetterhorn Hotel in Hasliberg is made using fresh Alpine hay and follows a decades-old recipe that was recently found in the hotel basement.

Iva

Iva *Schnaps* has been made for centuries in Graubünden from the Iva plant (Iva in Rumantsch, with the romantic English name of simple leaved milfoil). Its scientific name is *Achillea moschata Wulfen*, and it is a subspecies of milfoil, or yarrow, that happily grows 2000 m/6562 ft above sea level. Initially made in private homes, it was the *Zuckerbäcker*— the intrepid young men who left their rustic upbringings to traverse the continent working in bakeries and pastry shops—who commercialized the drink and sold it on their travels.

Bottom left, Andi Brechbühl

A Visit to Mia Iva

To get to Tschlin, you have to go to the very ends of Switzerland.

Nestled in the mountains just before the Austrian border, Tschlin is so small that it's recommended you park your car outside the town and enter on foot. The houses are in the typical Engadin style; some white-washed with Sgraffito designs etched into the external walls. There is a large dairy, and as we passed in front, we saw a fountain full of big milk cans being kept cool in the afternoon sun.

Locals have been steeping Iva in their drinks for centuries, and for the last few years Andi Brechbühl has too. His company, Mia Iva, is located in the middle of the town, and it makes Iva to be sold commercially.

Originally from the Emmental, his background in agronomy and food production took him around the world—everywhere from Berlin to Marrakesh—before he settled in the most remote part of Switzerland with his family.

"We like it here," Andi says with a smile.

And he likes Iva.

"When you arrive at someone's house, you have an Iva," he says. "When you celebrate something, you have an Iva. And at the end of the meal, you probably need an Iva. It's something you drink together—a drink of friendship."

Although it was popular at home, it wasn't easy to buy in a shop; so, Andi decided to start bottling it. He harvests all the Iva plants himself in the summer, and over the years has found his perfect recipe. He steeps the plants in pure alcohol, then later adds a mix of water and sugar. Right after bottling, the liquid is wonderfully green, though the color mellows a bit with time.

The locals still make their own Iva, of course—it's a part of their culture—and they have feelings and questions about Andi's version. "What's his recipe? Does he use leaves AND flowers? Or just leaves? Or just flowers?" But they are slowly coming around to his version of the drink.

"They'll come to me if they don't have time to make their own—"

"—and buy a bottle?" I interrupt.

"No," he laughs, "just to get a few plants."

Raselli—Switzerland's Alpine Herb Garden

It's a sunny October afternoon in the Val Poschiavo, a valley high in the Alps of Graubünden, but so close to the border that the language spoken is Italian. The smell of peppermint is overwhelming.

"Get in," says Reto Raselli, motioning to an old but serviceable car, "and I'll show you the fields."

Reto Raselli has been growing herbs in the Val Poschiavo since the 1990s. His eponymous company is Switzerland's number one producer of organic herbs. Its 20-odd varieties have provided flavor to everything from Ricola throat lozenges to organic teas from Coop.

"We pull the weeds by hand," he says, as we roll past a field of sage. "It's one of our biggest challenges." Organic since the beginning, Raselli is committed to the best and most biodiverse agriculture. He runs the herb production, while his nephew runs a traditional farm nearby with animals, benefitting both.

Everything is grown within a 1 km/0.62 mi radius on about 14 hectares of land—incredible for the amount the company makes. But herbs are small, and most of them keep producing throughout the growing season, so a lot comes from a little land.

The company itself is also small, with only 10 employees who do most of the work by hand—save for some very cool packaging machines which make both traditional and pyramid-shaped tea bags. In fact, it is the only company in the country that cultivates its tea and bags it onsite.

In recent years, Raselli has been marketing its own teas more, and with the striking packaging using bold colors and animals, they have been a hit.

"My daughter asks for the owl tea," I tell him, referencing their evening tea with lemon balm and Alpine herbs.

He laughs. "Yes, kids typically ask for them by animal or color."

Along with these family favorites, there are the herbal mixes, and loose-leaf teas too. You can also buy bags of herbs like oregano and thyme, and colorful packages of edible flowers. And which tea is Reto Raselli's favorite? The Alpine herb tea with Edelweiss, which the company also cultivates, just next to its office.

Our tour goes past a few fields, many of which have already been harvested—it is October after all—but some of them are still green. The peppermint smell is still in the air, mixed with the scent of the mountains. With the lake and the Alps in the background, it looks, and smells, like paradise.

Top, Reto Raselli

Appenzeller Alpenbitter Distillery, canton Appenzell Innerrhoden

Bitter Drinks

Alpenbitter is a strong, bitter spirit flavored with herbs—perfectly combining the Swiss love of Alpine meadows and herbal remedies.

The first major Swiss *Alpenbitter* was Dennler-Bitter, founded by pharmacist August F. Dennler. He had been investigating digestion aides and rigorously tested his bitter solution. The only drink at the time that wouldn't turn cloudy when water was added, his *Magenbitter*, as it was called, soon became popular around the country—and the world. By the 20th century it was being exported to North America, Australia and Asia. Although the company went bust in the 1920s, Dennler set the standard for a good-tasting, effective *Alpenbitter* that claimed to settle the stomach too.

Appenzeller Alpenbitter

It was an Appenzeller, Emil Ebneter, who would eventually create Switzerland's most famous *Alpenbitter*. At the turn of the 20th century, Ebneter was busy experimenting with different local herbs, as he was interested in their medicinal properties. He opened up a shop, patented the name, joined forces with his brother-in-law Beat Kölbener, and relocated to a bigger distillery location (the same as today). He asked his local monks to lend their herbal know-how, and ended up winning the gold medal for his bitter at the Swiss Expo in 1914.

The company remains a family affair, and today just one member of each family (Ebneter and Kölbener) knows the secret recipe.

BOTTOMS UP!

You can drink Appenzeller Alpenbitter right from the source at their factory in the picturesque Swiss city of Appenzell. Take a trip into their *Kräuterwelt* (herb world) to learn about the 42 herbs they use in their brew, or simply walk the path just outside the factory shop where you can see all the plants growing.

Bitter des Diablerets

Although Appenzeller is undoubtedly the most famous of all the Swiss *Alpenbitters*, other versions are made throughout the country, with each producer using their own distinct mix of herbs.

One such example is Bitter des Diablerets. Its legend goes like this: in the 18th century, the devil thought he would amuse himself by throwing rocks, causing landslides in the tiny village of Derborence, high in the Valais. The village was destroyed, but the peasants survived by sucking the Alpine herbs that were growing on the fallen rocks. The mountains were renamed Diablerets (home of the devil) after their cloven-footed foe, and the bitters, made with those same Alpine herbs, took on this name as well.

Bitter des Diablerets can be drunk alone or mixed with cola or other fizzy drinks. Mixed with the classic Swiss soda Elmer Citro (use Sprite or 7UP if you can't find Elmer), it's citrusy with a bitter bite.

Glarner Alpenbitter

The canton of Glarus makes its own *Alpenbitter* too, and its history is equally long and storied. The well-known priest and naturopath Johann Künzle developed a bitter herbal drink in 1918, intended to combat and prevent the spread of the Spanish flu. And if anyone knew herbs, it was Künzle. He wrote two bestselling books about healing plants: *Chrut & Uchrut*, which is still in print, and an atlas of medicinal herbs, which sold over a million copies.

Initially sold throughout the country, Künzle's *Alpenbitter* was a success. But once its parent company was sold, it disappeared from the market... until 2014, when an enthusiastic group of Glarners, who wanted to promote and sell traditional products from Glarus, brought it back to life. Now you can find it in stores in the region and online.

Weisflog

It was German implant Gustav Weisflog, a specialist in stomach troubles, who developed this alkaline bitter in Zurich in 1880. Initially meant to treat stomach acidity, it eventually also came to be enjoyed as an aperitif. Still being sold today, its recipe remains unchanged.

DIABLE AMER

150 ml/5 fl oz Elmer Citro or other lemonade

Stir with ice.

60 ml/2 fl oz Bitter des Diablerets

30 ml/1 fl oz lime juice

MITTEDRINK

My friends at zur Alten Weinhandlung in Trubschachen like their *Alpenbitter* with a dash of the green fairy and a smoky branch of rosemary to boot.

60 ml/2 fl oz Alpenbitter (preferably Glarner)
20 ml/0.7 fl oz absinthe
A rosemary branch

Stir the *Alpenbitter* and absinthe with ice. To garnish, lightly toast the branch of rosemary with a match, then swirl it into the drink.

ALPENBITTER NEGRONI

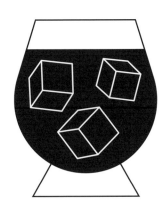

Amateur mixologist and professional brain scientist Dr Richard McKinley introduced me to this version of a Negroni, which swaps out Campari for *Alpenbitter*.

30 ml/1 fl oz gin
30 ml/1 fl oz sweet vermouth
30 ml/1 fl oz Alpenbitter

Stir with ice.

ALPENBITTER EISKAFFEE

Vanilla or coffee ice cream
200 ml/¾ cup freshly brewed coffee, cooled slightly
30 ml/2 tbsp Alpenbitter
Whipped cream

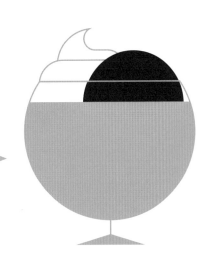

Place a large scoop of vanilla or coffee ice cream into a large mug or glass. Top with the coffee and *Alpenbitter*. Stir well and garnish with whipped cream.

Top right, Barb Grossenbacher

Edelwhite Gin—Alpine Herbs from the Biosphere

If you think mobile distilleries are a thing of the past, think again. When Barb Grossenbacher needed to distill some gin she approached Bruno Limacher, a local with a mobile distillery, and asked him to make four bottles.

"Four? My still holds 350 liters (92 gallons)! How about 300 bottles?"

"I don't have enough friends and family!" said Barb; but soon she relented, and the first batch of Edelwhite Gin was distilled. Within six weeks it had won a bronze medal at the International Wine and Spirit Competition (IWSC) in London and Lucerne's biggest newspaper, the *Luzerner Zeitung*, wanted an interview.

"Where is your distillery? In the laundry room? The cellar? The garage?" asked the journalist.

Barb hadn't banked on becoming a gin maker. She had worked decades in the hospitality industry—first where she'd grown up, in Canada, washing dishes at the Jasper Park Lodge. That's where she met a Swiss chef, Fritz, who would become her husband. They both worked throughout Switzerland, eventually running their own hotel.

However, when approaching 50, she knew she wanted something different. With a long interest in wine and spirits, she decided to study for her WSET (Wine and Spirits Educational Trust) diploma as a wine academic. "From Botanicals to the Bottle" was the title of her final project, and she made her own gin. With support from her friend Sandra, an expert herbalist, the women developed a recipe using 27 herbs—14 local to the UNESCO Biosphere Entlebuch where they lived.

The business grew and the women strove to better their bronze medal, entering different spirit competitions around the world. Sadly, around this time Sandra got sick. Just as Edelwhite won gold at the IWSC and was voted best gin in the world in 2019, Sandra died of breast cancer.

Sandra still remains an integral part of the company. Visiting the Edelwhite distillery, I notice a little angel figure sitting on top of the still. Barb shows me the big sacks of botanicals, the ones she and Sandra tested over a hundred times to get right. "Smell this," she says, indicating a big bag of dried Edelweiss. The furry Swiss flowers smell like hay.

Although tinged with sadness, Barb's experience of becoming a gin maker seems like fate.

"You know, my maiden name is White," she says, with a smile.

Today, Edelwhite Gin is sold all over Switzerland and Barb offers not just her traditional gin with the unchanged, award-winning recipe that she and Sandra developed in 2017, but also a navy-strength gin for gin-lovers at 57%, an orange gin, vodka, and an excellent cheese fondue-mix with gin. You can visit the distillery and, under Barb's careful eye, make your own gin, too.

Chapter 10: From the Trees

ARVENSCHNAPS

The woodsy, pine smell from many Alpine dwellings often comes from furniture (or the walls) made from *Pinus cembra* or *Arven* (Swiss pine). This tree, which grows throughout the Alps and Carpathian Mountains, has been known for centuries to have therapeutic properties. Even sleeping in a bed made from its wood is said to lower your heart rate. Of course, its curative properties can also be imbibed, and many Alpine dwellers, especially those in Graubünden, make spirits from both its buds and its pinecones.

3-4 pinecones from a Swiss pine tree
500 ml/2 cups kirsch

In late June/early July, harvest 3-4 pinecones from a Swiss pine tree, *Pinus cembra*. Rinse the pinecones, slice into rounds and place in a large glass jar with the kirsch. Cover and leave in a warm place for a few months. Strain and pour into a bottle.

TANNENSPITZ LIQUEUR

The soft, fragrant tips of the fir tree make an aromatic, lightly sour liqueur. The buds of the tree can be collected in April or May (though this will vary depending on your growing season and altitude). Before you collect your buds, make sure you are collecting from the right kind of tree: fir (not pine or spruce). Here's how to tell the difference: fir needles are soft and flat, while pine needles grow in clusters, and spruce needles are round and sharp.

2 handfuls of fir tree buds
Peel of half a lemon
500 ml/2 cups clear spirit, like kirsch
80 g/3 oz sugar
80 g/3 oz water

Rinse the pine tree buds under cold water and place in a large jar with the lemon peel. Add the spirit and mix well. Leave for about two weeks in the sun, shaking once every day or so.

After two weeks, strain the buds, reserving the spirit. Place the sugar and water in a pot, bring to a boil, and when all the sugar has dissolved remove from heat and let cool. Add to the spirit, mix well and bottle.

Nocino

Nocino is a bittersweet liqueur made from green walnuts and particularly enjoyed in Ticino. Though it's not unique to that region, it's possible that it has been produced there in monasteries since the 1500s. Walnut spirits are popular throughout Europe, and the Ticinese variety was probably introduced from Italy.

Like Ticino's famous chestnuts, walnuts also grow plentifully in Italian-speaking Switzerland (even up to an altitude of 1200 m/3937 ft), and at one time they were an essential product. Walnut oil was used not only for cooking, but also as lamp oil. The advent of electricity and availability of other cooking oils may have slowed the distribution of the trees, but also freed up more nuts to be used for booze.

Nocino is made by soaking green walnuts in spirit until the liquid turns black and bitter, then adding sugar and spices to make a complex, nutty, bittersweet drink. The nuts are only green for a short window of time, and traditionally the monks would make their batches on the same day every year: the eve of the Feast of St John on June 24. That's when they would harvest the unripe nuts and set to work steeping.

Sometimes Nocino is referred to as *ratafià*, which is actually a larger category of drinks, and seems to encompass many different spirits created by soaking fruits, nuts, and spices. The word *ratafià* comes from the Latin *rata fiat* (done deal, ratified) and signified the spirit that was imbibed after a contract or agreement had been signed.

Drinks with Nocino

NOCINO ALEXANDER

60 ml/2 fl oz rum
30 ml/1 fl oz Nocino
30 ml/1 fl oz cream
10 ml/0.3 fl oz cinnamon syrup
Cinnamon to garnish

Shake over ice
and pour into
a glass. Sprinkle
with cinnamon.

GREEN VALLEY

50 ml/1.7 fl oz Nocino
25 ml/0.8 fl oz absinthe
25 ml/0.8 fl oz Crème de Cassis
1 squeeze lemon juice
Dash of bitters

Shake over ice
and strain into
a martini glass.

Green walnuts
meet the green
fairy (and taste
like liquorice
allsorts).

NOCINO TODDY

50 ml/3 tbsp Nocino
1 tsp honey
Juice of half a lemon
Cinnamon tea

Place in a mug
and fill to the top
with cinnamon tea
(or hot water).

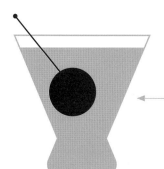

NOCINO MANHATTAN

50 ml/1.7 fl oz bourbon
20 ml/0.7 fl oz sweet
  vermouth
20 ml/0.7 fl oz Nocino
3 dashes bitters

Stir all ingredients together
and serve with ice. Garnish
with cherries.

Making Your Own Nocino

In many parts of Switzerland, you can forage your own green walnuts, which are usually ready for steeping in late June. They are ready to use if you can easily pierce the skin with a knife.

When you slice through a green walnut, the liquid released is clear, but don't let that fool you—green walnuts produce a powerful dye. Just as the Nocino will turn nearly black, so will everything that comes in contact with the liquid from the nuts, especially cutting boards and fingers. Be sure to cover up surfaces and wear rubber gloves.

Some Italian folklore suggests it is unlucky to make your Nocino with an even number of walnuts. Many recipes use grappa, but some people prefer high percent fruit brandies like kirsch or pure alcohol.

NOCINO

21 green walnuts
500 g/2½ cups sugar
1 liter/4 cups clear spirit
Half a cinnamon stick
1 clove
1 coffee bean
1 small strip of lemon peel
* (no bigger than your pinkie)*

Cut each walnut into quarters and put into a large, wide-mouth jar. Add the sugar, close and shake well. Place in the sun for two days, shaking often.

After two days, you will see that lots of liquid has seeped out of the nuts. Now you can add the flavorings and alcohol. Don't be tempted to add more flavorings—a little goes a long way.

Let sit in a partially sunny place for 60 days.

Filter into dark bottles through cheesecloth or fine mesh. Store in a cool place. The Nocino should be left for at least a year before being drunk, in order for the tannins (which make the drink bitter) to soften and the full flavor to develop.

Swiss Flip (recipe on page 138)

Chapter 11: From the Bars

Switzerland has some very famous bars. Just look at the Kronenhalle in Zurich, one that hosted the likes of James Joyce, Pablo Picasso, Andy Warhol, Catherine Deneuve, Plácido Domingo, Coco Chanel and Lauren Bacall—even Swiss literary kings Friedrich Dürrenmatt and Max Frisch were regulars.

In 1984, Kronenhalle head bartender Peter Roth developed the Ladykiller, a strong fruity drink that won the world cocktail award and made its way into the canon.

LADYKILLER

30 ml/1 fl oz gin
15 ml/0.5 fl oz Cointreau
15 ml/0.5 fl oz apricot brandy
60 ml/2 fl oz pineapple juice
60 ml/2 fl oz passionfruit juice

Shake with ice. Strain into a long drink glass with ice. If you order this at the Kronenhalle, it might be garnished with orange slices formed into a rose, perched on peppermint leaves.

Harry Schraemli

There was really only one man who worked tirelessly to bring American cocktail culture to Switzerland, and his name was Harry Schraemli.

Alongside a long career in the hospitality industry (at 26 he was the youngest hotel manager of his time), he also wrote passionately about food and drink. Most notable is his *Das Grosse Lehrbuch der Bar* (The Big Bar Manual), first published in the 1940s, which became the standard book for Swiss hospitality students to learn mixology and bartending.

In the book, Schraemli lays out everything you need for the smooth handling of a bar—an inventory of correct glasses, suggestions for modest food offerings, what to look for in bar staff, how to stock a wine cellar, a selection of toasts in English, descriptions of pretty much every bottled drink that existed at the time, and recipes for all standard cocktails, plus a few creations of his own.

My favorite Schraemli drink is his delicious Violetta cocktail.

VIOLETTA

30 ml/1 fl oz Crème de Cassis
30 ml/1 fl oz cream
60 ml/2 fl oz Eierkirsch

Shake with ice and strain into a glass.

Here are two more Swiss-themed cocktail favorites from Harry Schraemli's famous book. He describes the Flip as a drink that can be enjoyed in the morning and one favored by women and convalescents. You can leave out the yolk if you like, but if you use one, serve and drink immediately.

SWISS FLIP

1 egg yolk
2 tsp sugar
30 ml/1 fl oz cherry liqueur
30 ml/1 fl oz Pflümli
1 tbsp instant coffee
60 ml/2 fl oz cream

Shake with ice, strain into a glass and garnish with a little more instant coffee.

RADIO SUISSE COCKTAIL

30 ml/1 fl oz apricot brandy
30 ml/1 fl oz pineapple juice
Champagne or sparkling wine
Orange to garnish

Shake the brandy and pineapple juice with ice. Strain into a champagne glass and top with champagne or sparkling wine. Garnish with an orange slice.

Sours

So many of Switzerland's fruit and nut spirits and liqueurs are perfect for making sours. Frothy, sweet and sour, these cocktails go down a treat. Traditionally these drinks are made with a raw egg white, which gives them a rich mouthfeel and foamy topping, but you can also leave this out completely, or use pasteurized egg whites or aquafaba (chickpea water) if you prefer. Each drink serves one, but the recipes can easily be doubled.

KIRSCH SOUR

60 ml/2 fl oz kirsch
30 ml/1 fl oz lemon juice
20 ml/0.7 fl oz cherry syrup or
  Röteli
15 ml/0.5 fl oz egg white

PLUM SOUR

60 ml/2 fl oz Zwetschgen
30 ml/1 fl oz lemon juice
20 ml/0.7 fl oz cinnamon syrup
15 ml/0.5 fl oz egg white

PEAR SOUR

60 ml/2 fl oz Williams
30 ml/1 fl oz lemon juice
20 ml/0.7 fl oz elderflower syrup
15 ml/0.5 fl oz egg white

NOCINO SOUR

60 ml/2 fl oz Nocino
30 ml/1 fl oz lemon juice
15 ml/0.5 fl oz egg white
Dash of bitters

If you use egg whites, shake the ingredients in the cocktail shaker first without ice, then add the ice and shake again (this creates the best foam). Otherwise, just shake everything with ice.

15 ml/0.5 fl oz egg white is about 1 tbsp/half an egg white (though if I'm making just one drink, I usually throw in the entire white for extra frothiness).

Puttin' on the Ritz

César Ritz, born in 1850 in Niederwald, Valais, was the last of 13 children and extremely poor. With ingenuity and exacting standards, he went from those humble beginnings to having his name be a synonym for unabashed luxury.

From waiter to hotel manager, anecdotal stories about his resourcefulness abound. While managing a hotel on the Rigi-Kulm, the heating went out just before a lunch for 40 wealthy American guests. To warm the room he had copper palm pots emptied, filled with oil, and lit on fire. Then he placed warm, blanket-wrapped bricks at the feet of each guest.

But his inventiveness wasn't just focused on the wealthy. Shortly before the opening of the Grand Hotel in Rome, the workers went on strike, so Ritz organized a dinner for them on the site of the ballroom (with plenty of Chianti and charcuterie) and they were back at work the following day.

He championed hygienic practices in hotels and his were the very first to have private ensuite bathrooms in each room. To flatter the complexions and accent the jewelry of his clients, he used indirect lighting, as well as pale peach and gold tones that still exist in many Ritz dining rooms today. Less flattering was an incident with King Edward VII, who got stuck in the bathtub he was sharing with a lady, leading Ritz to invent a king-sized tub for his portly guest.

It was Ritz who supposedly gave Grand Marnier its name, so it's fitting that it features in his own luxury cocktail.

Want to make your Ritz particularly memorable? Flame the orange peel.

This technique was favored by Dale DeGroff who used to make the drink in New York's Rainbow Room in the 1980s. Cut a five-franc-sized (3 cm/1 in) circle from the peel of an orange. With the orange peel facing away from you, light a match, then squeeze the peel so that the oils spray through the flame. You'll get a little blaze, and then you can drop the peel into the drink.

THE RITZ

60 ml/2 fl oz cognac
30 ml/1 fl oz Grand Marnier
30 ml/1 fl oz orange juice
Champagne

Shake the cognac, Grand Marnier and orange juice with ice and strain into a champagne glass. Top with champagne.

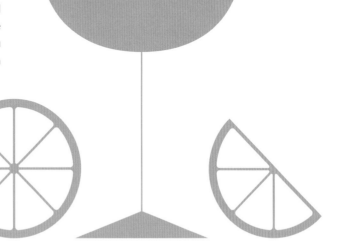

Chapter 12: From the Slopes

The combinations of booze, sugar, warm liquid and cream served on Swiss ski hills are endless. Whether you drink them for aprés-ski or skip the skiing altogether, these cozy, spirited concoctions are bound to warm your belly.

The recipes are calculated to make single servings of around 200 ml/7 fl oz (the size of a standard Swiss coffee glass), except for the *Jägertee*, which is made in a large mug.

SCHÜMLI PFLÜMLI

30 ml/1 fl oz Pflümli, or other plum brandy
2 tsp sugar
150 ml/5 fl oz hot, strong coffee
Whipped cream and chocolate powder to garnish

Mix together the brandy and sugar in your coffee glass or mug. Top with hot coffee and lots of whipped cream and chocolate powder.

BOMBARDINO

This one comes from Italy, but it's a favorite on the Swiss slopes as well.

100 ml/3.4 fl oz hot milk
1 tsp sugar
50 ml/1.7 fl oz Eierkirsch
30 ml/1 fl oz whiskey or brandy
Whipped cream and cinnamon to
    garnish

Mix together the sugar and hot milk in a coffee glass or mug. Add the *Eierkirsch* and brandy, and top with whipped cream and a sprinkle of cinnamon.

SCHOGGI MIT SCHUSS

Schoggi, the Swiss German word for chocolate, gets a *Schuss* (shot) of something spirited.

150 ml/5 fl oz hot chocolate
50 ml/1.7 fl oz spirit of your
    choosing
Whipped cream

Mix together the hot chocolate and booze and garnish with lots of whipped cream. Some good spirits are rum, whiskey, Baileys, amaretto, Nocino, or Cointreau.

KAFI BIBERFLADE

30 ml/1 fl oz Appenzeller Alpenbitter
1 tsp sugar
150 ml/5 fl oz hot coffee
Whipped cream

Mix together the *Alpenbitter* and sugar in your coffee glass or mug. Top with hot coffee and garnish with whipped cream. Tastes best with an Appenzeller *Biberli* (a soft cookie filled with marzipan) on the side.

HOLDRIO

30 ml/1 fl oz Zwetschgen or other
    plum brandy
2 sugar cubes (or 2 tsp sugar)
150 ml/5 fl oz rose hip tea

Mix together the brandy and sugar in a coffee glass or mug. Top with hot tea.

Schoggi mit Schuss

Holdrio

JÄGERTEE

German for hunter's tea, it's similar to *Glühwein*, only caffeinated.

30 ml/1 fl oz rum
1 tsp sugar
100 ml/3.4 fl oz red wine
200 ml/6.7 fl oz hot black tea
  (brewed with a clove and
  cinnamon stick)

Mix together the rum and sugar in a large mug. Add the red wine and hot black tea and stir well.

GLETSCHERWASSER

With no cream or sugar to hide behind, this packs a warm, tart punch.

50 ml/1.7 fl oz Zwetschgen or
  other plum brandy
50 ml/1.7 fl oz lemon juice
100 ml/3.4 fl oz hot water

Mix together in a coffee glass or mug. Garnish with a lemon slice.

GÜGGELBRUNZ

In Swiss German, this drink's name means rooster's urine.

150 ml/5 fl oz hot peppermint tea
50 ml/1.7 fl oz Zwetschgen (or
  other plum brandy)

Mix together in a coffee glass or mug.

FÜDLIWÄRMER

Füdli is the Swiss German word for bum or bottom.

2 sugar cubes
15 ml/0.5 fl oz Abricotine
15 ml/0.5 fl oz Träsch
15 ml/0.5 fl oz Zwetschgen
150 ml/5 fl oz hot coffee

Mix together the *Schnaps* and sugar in your coffee glass or mug. Top with hot coffee.

Flämmli

The stakes are higher with a *Flämmli*, especially if you've already had a few. It's basically a boozy coffee, set alight. A poorly orchestrated one probably won't result in scorched eyebrows, but it might split your cup clean in half.

Williams is the traditional spirit, but other high-proof varieties work too.

How to serve Flämmli without cracking your cup

- Add two teaspoons of sugar or two sugar cubes to an espresso—DO NOT STIR.

- Drink the espresso, leaving the sugar, undissolved, at the bottom of the cup.

- Add a shot of Williams, then dip your spoon into the booze and lift up a spoonful. Using a match or lighter, set it on fire and tip the flaming booze back into the cup—but watch out, it will flame up! Then spoon the sugar from the bottom of the cup into the flame to caramelize it.

- Put the flame out with the saucer of the cup or, if you're feeling brave, your flat palm. Let cool, then drink.

Resources

There are many great resources if you're interested in learning about Swiss drinks and drinking culture. Here are some that I used while researching this book.

The Swiss government website lists all the statistics related to beverage consumption, as well as an archive of laws relating to alcohol. In 2016, they published a detailed book *Rausch & Ordnung/Ivresse & Ordre/Ebbrezza e Ordine*, about the entire history of the Swiss Alcohol Board (1887–2015). It's filled with photos, statistics, and meticulous history, and can be ordered on the government's website.

Harry Schraemli, Switzerland's consummate barkeep and educator, literally wrote the textbook on bar culture in the 20th century. It's called *Das Grosse Lehrbuch der Bar*.

Kurt Lussi's book *Liebestrünke: Mythen, Riten, Rezepte* is a fascinating look at love potions and home remedies throughout the ages, in Switzerland and further afield.

For more on apple (and pear) cider in many forms, particularly around Lake Lucerne, there's Heiri Scherer's *Most*.

Marianne Kaltenbach, Switzerland's premier food chronicler, wrote about many drinks in her *Aus Schweizer Küchen*.

Baden und Trinken in den Bergen: Heilquellen in Graubünden, by Karin Fuchs, is a fascinating look at the canton's many mineral spas and sanatoriums.

If you'd like to take a closer look at the history of the Green Fairy, check out the award-winning *Absinthe, The Forbidden Spirit*, by Tania Brasseur and Tamara Berger.

Want to hike the Swiss vineyards? There's no better guide than *Wine Hiking Switzerland* by Ellen Wallace.

And finally, there is the online Culinary Heritage of Switzerland (*Kulinarisches Erbe der Schweiz/Patrimoine Culinaire Suisse/Patrimonio Culinario Svizzero*): an astounding collection of information about traditional and historic Swiss food and drink products.

Recipe Tips

For the recipes that mention shaking, you will need a cocktail shaker and ice.

When making infused spirits or syrups, use clean bottles. You can sterilize them by boiling them in hot water for 10 minutes or running them through the dishwasher. Syrups keep in the fridge for a few weeks and spirits will keep in the liquor cabinet almost indefinitely.

When straining syrups, use a metal sieve, but with the infused spirits your best bet is cheesecloth or another very fine mesh.

My default *Schnaps* base is a standard kirsch, which has little flavor. You can also use other high-alcohol, low-flavor spirits like vodka or *Träsch*.

Acknowledgments

Cheers to everyone who helped make this book possible!

What a dream it is to work with Richard and the team at Helvetiq and Bergli—special thanks to Shona, Eleni, Ela, Karin, and Angela for all your help.

I had such a wonderful time visiting drink producers throughout the country.

Viva! to Andi Brechbühl at Mia Iva, for a wonderful afternoon in the sun. Cheers to the marvelous Barb Grossenbacher from Edelwhite Gin, it was a delight to get to know you better! Thanks, eh? *Cin-cin*, Herr Raselli, and thank you for a wonderful visit in the beautiful Val Poschiavo (from Stella too!). *Proscht* to Basti Degen! Thank you for your time! *Zum Wohl* to the team at Mosterei Kobelt—it was a real joy to visit your lovely little cidery. Thank you, Jonathan, and the rest of the team from Distillery Studer. It's always a pleasure to visit! And *Proscht* to Robert Schröter for the wonderful Swiss drink!

Danke to Hanna Stalder for your knowledge about the *Brächete* and *Brächere Brönnts*, and to Anna Katharina Meyer, Sonja Feuz and the other participants. Thanks to David and Johanna for insight into the Romandie, and to Heddi for reminding me about municipal wine. Thank you, Barbara, for the tips on *Holdrio*, and thanks to Vreni for your knowledge about Ticino.

Friedrich, thank you for your reflections on *Äntlibuecher Kafi*. It's always a joy to drink with you and your family.

Richard—thanks for preparing my first-ever breakfast martini with jam. Here's to being one of the best, and classiest, drinking buddies ever. Same goes for you Mary—and here's to much more merrymaking (and thank you for your sharp editor's eye).

Uncle Stuart, thank you so much for your invaluable editing. The next round's on me.

Thank you Fränzi, for everything (not only the booze). I always think of you *when ich muess, ich muess, ich muess es Schnäpseli ha*. Thank you to my parents-in-law, Robi and Josy—I have learned so much from you and I am so grateful for your support. Thanks for all the *Milchkaffee*. Mom, thanks for decades of Ov(om)altine and chamomile tea, and thank you for always taking such good care of us.

Cheers, Sam for showing me the wide world of whiskey, sour beer, and yogi drinks (in that order), and for winning me over to the good coffee maker. Your sloe gin is legendary.

And finally, a hearty *Zum Wohl* to Stella! Whether *Most* or mocktail, she's a girl who knows a good varnish.

Index